THE ULTIMATE FOUNDATION OF ECONOMIC SCIENCE

An Essay on Method

Titles in the Liberty Fund Library of the Works of
Ludwig von Mises

LUDWIG VON MISES

The Ultimate Foundation of Economic Science

An Essay on Method

∿ LUDWIG VON MISES

Edited by Bettina Bien Greaves

LIBERTY FUND   *Indianapolis*

Editorial Additions © 2006 Liberty Fund, Inc.

Front cover photograph of Ludwig von Mises used by permission of the Ludwig von Mises Institute, Auburn, Alabama.

Frontispiece courtesy of Bettina Bien Greaves

First published in 1962 by William Volker Fund in association with D. Van Nostrand, Inc. The second edition was published in 1978 by the Institute for Humane Studies, Inc. In 2002, Bettina Bien Greaves reprinted the second edition in association with the Foundation for Economic Education.

Printed in the United States of America

| 10 | 09 | 08 | 07 | 06 | C | 5 | 4 | 3 | 2 | 1 |
| 10 | 09 | 08 | 07 | 06 | P | 5 | 4 | 3 | 2 | 1 |

Library of Congress Cataloging-in-Publication Data
Von Mises, Ludwig, 1881–1973.
  The ultimate foundation of economic science: an essay on method/ Ludwig von Mises.—2nd ed.
        p.   cm.—(Liberty Fund library of the works of Ludwig von Mises)
    "The second edition was published in 1978 by the Institute for Humane Studies, Inc. In 2002, Bettina Bien Greaves reprinted the second edition in association with the Foundation for Economic Education"—T.p. verso.
    Includes bibliographical references and index.
    ISBN-13: 978-0-86597-638-2 (hardcover: alk. paper)
    ISBN-10: 0-86597-638-4 (hardcover: alk. paper)
    ISBN-13: 978-0-86597-639-9 (pbk.: alk. paper)
    ISBN-10: 0-86597-639-2 (pbk.: alk. paper)
    1. Economics.   2. Economics—Methodology.   3. Positivism.
    I. Title.   II. Series: Von Mises, Ludgwig, 1881–1973.   Works.   2005.
HB71.V65   2006
330.01—dc22   2005033274

Liberty Fund, Inc.
8335 Allison Pointe Trail, Suite 300
Indianapolis, Indiana 46250-1684

CONTENTS

This essay is not a contribution to philosophy. It is merely the exposition of certain ideas that attempts to deal with the theory of knowledge ought to take into full account.

Traditional logic and epistemology have produced, by and large, merely disquisitions on mathematics and the methods of the natural sciences. The philosophers considered physics as the paragon of science and blithely assumed that all knowledge is to be fashioned on its model. They dispensed with biology, satisfying themselves that one day later generations would succeed in reducing the phenomena of life to the operation of elements that can be fully described by physics. They slighted history as "mere literature" and ignored the existence of economics. Positivism, as foreshadowed by Laplace, baptized by Auguste Comte, and resuscitated and systematized by contemporary logical or empirical positivism, is essentially pan-physicalism, a scheme to deny that there is any other method of scientific thinking than that starting from the physicist's recording of "protocol sentences." Its materialism encountered opposition only on the part of metaphysicians who freely indulged in the invention of fictitious entities and of arbitrary systems of what they called "philosophy of history."

This essay proposes to stress the fact that there is in the universe something for the description and analysis of which the natural sciences cannot contribute anything. There are events beyond the range of those events that the procedures of the natural sciences are fit to observe and to describe. There is human action.

It is a fact that up to now nothing has been done to bridge over the gulf that yawns between the natural events in the consummation of which science is unable to find any finality and the conscious acts of men that invariably aim at definite ends. To neglect, in the treatment of human action, reference to the ends aimed at by the actors is no less absurd than were the endeavors to resort to finality in the interpretation of natural phenomena.

It would be a mistake to insinuate that all the errors concerning the epistemological interpretation of the sciences of human action are to be ascribed to the unwarranted adoption of the epistemology of positivism. There were other schools of thought that confused the philosophical treatment of praxeology and history even more seriously than positivism, e.g., historicism. Yet, the following analysis deals first of all with the impact of positivism.[1]

In order to avoid misinterpretation of the point of view of this essay, it is advisable, even necessary, to stress the fact that it deals with knowledge, science, and reasonable belief and that it refers to metaphysical doctrines only as far as it is necessary to demonstrate in what respects they differ from scientific knowledge. It unreservedly endorses Locke's principle of "not entertaining any proposition with greater assurance than the proofs it is built upon will warrant." The viciousness of positivism is not to be seen in the adoption of this principle, but in the fact that it does not acknowledge any other ways of proving a proposition than those practiced by the experimental natural sciences and qualifies as metaphysical — which, in the positivist jargon, is synonymous with nonsensical — all other methods of rational discourse. To expose the fallaciousness of this fundamental thesis of positivism and to depict its disastrous consequences is the only theme of this essay.

Although full of contempt for all it considers as metaphysics, the epistemology of positivism is itself based upon a definite brand of metaphysics. It is beyond the pale of a rational inquiry to enter into an analysis of any variety of metaphysics, to try to appraise its value or its tenability and to affirm or to reject it. What discursive reasoning can achieve is merely to show whether or not the metaphysical doctrine in question contradicts what has been established as scientifically proved truth. If this can be demonstrated with regard to positivism's assertions concerning the sciences of human action, its claims are to be rejected as unwarranted fables. The positivists themselves, from the point of view of their own philosophy, could not help but approve of such a verdict.

General epistemology can be studied only by those who are perfectly familiar with all branches of human knowledge. The special

---

1. About historicism, *see* Mises, *Theory and History* (New Haven: Yale University Press, 1957 [Auburn, Ala.: Ludwig von Mises Institute, 1985]), pp. 198 ff.

epistemological problems of the different fields of knowledge are accessible only to those who have a perfect acquaintance with the respective field. There would not be any need to mention this point if it were not for the shocking ignorance of everything concerning the sciences of human action that characterizes the writings of almost all contemporary philosophers.[2]

It may even be doubted whether it is possible to separate the analysis of epistemological problems from the treatment of the substantive issues of the science concerned. The basic contributions to the modern epistemology of the natural sciences were an accomplishment of Galilei, not of Bacon, of Newton and Lavoisier, not of Kant and Comte. What is tenable in the doctrines of logical positivism is to be found in the works of the great physicists of the last hundred years, not in the "Encyclopedia of Unified Science." My own contributions to the theory of knowledge, however modest they may be, are in my economic and historical writings, especially in my books *Human Action* and *Theory and History*. The present essay is merely a supplement to and a commentary on what economics itself says about its own epistemology.

He who seriously wants to grasp the purport of economic theory ought to familiarize himself first with what economics teaches and only then, having again and again reflected upon these theorems, turn to the study of the epistemological aspects concerned. Without a most careful examination of at least some of the great issues of praxeological thinking — as, e.g., the law of returns (mostly called the law of diminishing returns), the Ricardian law of association (better known as the law of comparative cost), the problem of economic calculation, and so on — nobody can expect to comprehend what praxeology means and what its specific epistemological problems involve.

---

2. A striking example of this ignorance displayed by an eminent philosopher, Henri Bergson, is quoted in Mises, *Human Action* (New Haven: Yale University Press, 1949 [4th ed., Irvington, N.Y.: Foundation for Economic Education, 1996]), p. 33 note.

THE ULTIMATE FOUNDATION OF
ECONOMIC SCIENCE

An Essay on Method

Some Preliminary Observations Concerning Praxeology Instead of an Introduction

1   The Permanent Substratum of Epistemology

Πάντα ῥεῖ, everything is in a ceaseless flux, says Heraclitus; there is no permanent being; all is change and becoming. It must be left to metaphysical speculation to deal with the problems whether this proposition can be borne out from the point of view of a superhuman intelligence and furthermore whether it is possible for a human mind to think of change without implying the concept of a substratum that, while it changes, remains in some regard and sense constant in the succession of its various states. For epistemology, the theory of human knowledge, there is certainly something that it cannot help considering as permanent, viz., the logical and praxeological structure of the human mind, on the one hand, and the power of the human senses, on the other hand. Fully aware of the fact that human nature as it is in this epoch of cosmic changes in which we are living is neither something that existed from the very beginning of all things nor something that will remain forever, epistemology must look upon it as if it were unchanging. The natural sciences may try to go further and to study the problems of evolution. But epistemology is a branch — or rather, the basis — of the sciences of man. It deals with one aspect of the nature of man as he emerged from the eons of cosmic becoming and as he is in this period of the history of the universe. It does not deal with thinking, perceiving and knowing in general, but with *human* thinking, perceiving and knowing. For epistemology there is something that it must take as unchanging, viz., the logical and praxeological structure of the human mind.

One must not confuse knowledge with mysticism. The mystic may say that "shadow and sunlight are the same."[1] Knowledge starts from the clear distinction between A and non-A.

1. R. W. Emerson, *Brahma.*

We know that there were ages of cosmic history in which there did not exist beings of the kind we call Homo sapiens, and we are free to assume that there will be again ages in which this species will not exist. But it is vain for us to speculate about the conditions of beings that are, in the logical and praxeological structure of their minds and in the power of their senses, essentially different from man as we know him and as we are ourselves. Nietzsche's concept of a superman is devoid of any epistemological meaning.

2 On Action

Epistemology deals with the mental phenomena of human life, with man as he thinks and acts. The main deficiency of traditional epistemological attempts is to be seen in their neglect of the praxeological aspects. The epistemologists dealt with thinking as if it were a separate field cut off from other manifestations of human endeavor. They dealt with the problems of logic and mathematics, but they failed to see the practical aspects of thinking. They ignored the praxeological a priori.

The shortcomings of this approach became manifest in the teachings of natural theology as distinguished from revealed theology. Natural theology saw the characteristic mark of deity in freedom from the limitations of the human mind and the human will. Deity is omniscient and almighty. But in elaborating these ideas the philosophers failed to see that a concept of deity that implies an acting God, that is, a God behaving in the way man behaves in acting, is self-contradictory. Man acts because he is dissatisfied with the state of affairs as it prevails in the absence of his intervention. Man acts because he lacks the power to render conditions fully satisfactory and must resort to appropriate means in order to render them less unsatisfactory. But for an almighty supreme being there cannot be any dissatisfaction with the prevailing state of affairs. The Almighty does not act, because there is no state of affairs that he cannot render fully satisfactory without any action, i.e., without resorting to any means. For Him there is no such thing as a distinction between ends and means. It is anthropomorphism to ascribe action to God. Starting from the limitations of his human nature, man's discursive reasoning can never circumscribe and define the essence of omnipotence.

However, it must be emphasized that what prevented people from paying attention to the praxeological issues was not theological considerations. It was the passionate longing for the realization of the utopian chimera of the land of Cockaigne. As the science of economics, the up-to-now best elaborated part of praxeology, exploded the fallacies of every brand of utopianism, it was outlawed and stigmatized as unscientific.

The most characteristic trait of modern epistemology is its entire neglect of economics, that branch of knowledge whose development and practical application was the most spectacular event of modern history.

3   On Economics

The study of economics has been again and again led astray by the vain idea that economics must proceed according to the pattern of other sciences. The mischief done by such misconstructions cannot be avoided by admonishing the economist to stop casting longing glances upon other fields of knowledge or even to ignore them entirely. Ignorance, whatever subject it may concern, is in no case a quality that could be useful in the search for truth. What is needed to prevent a scholar from garbling economic studies by resorting to the methods of mathematics, physics, biology, history or jurisprudence is not slighting and neglecting these sciences, but, on the contrary, trying to comprehend and to master them. He who wants to achieve anything in praxeology must be conversant with mathematics, physics, biology, history, and jurisprudence, lest he confuse the tasks and the methods of the theory of human action with the tasks and the methods of any of these other branches of knowledge. What was wrong with the various Historical Schools of economics was first of all that their adepts were merely dilettantes in the field of history. No competent mathematician can fail to see through the fundamental fallacies of all varieties of what is called mathematical economics and especially of econometrics. No biologist was ever fooled by the rather amateurish organicism of such authors as Paul de Lilienfeld.

When I once expressed this opinion in a lecture, a young man in the audience objected. "You are asking too much of an economist," he observed; "nobody can force me to employ my time in studying all these sciences." My answer was: "Nobody asks or forces you to become an economist."

4   The Starting Point of Praxeological Thinking

The a priori knowledge of praxeology is entirely different — categorially different — from the a priori knowledge of mathematics or, more precisely, from mathematical a priori knowledge as interpreted by logical positivism. The starting point of all praxeological thinking is not arbitrarily chosen axioms, but a self-evident proposition, fully, clearly and necessarily present in every human mind. An unbridgeable gulf separates those animals in whose minds this cognition is present from those in whose minds it is not fully and clearly present. Only to the former is the appellation man accorded. The characteristic feature of man is precisely that he consciously acts. Man is Homo agens, the acting animal.

All — apart from zoology — that has ever been scientifically stated to distinguish man from nonhuman mammals is implied in the proposition: man acts. To act means: to strive after ends, that is, to choose a goal and to resort to means in order to attain the goal sought.

The essence of logical positivism is to deny the cognitive value of a priori knowledge by pointing out that all a priori propositions are merely analytic. They do not provide new information, but are merely verbal or tautological, asserting what has already been implied in the definitions and premises. Only experience can lead to synthetic propositions. There is an obvious objection against this doctrine, viz., that this proposition that there are no synthetic a priori propositions is in itself a — as the present writer thinks, false — synthetic a priori proposition, for it can manifestly not be established by experience.

The whole controversy is, however, meaningless when applied to praxeology. It refers essentially to geometry. Its present state, especially its treatment by logical positivism, has been deeply influenced by the shock that Western philosophy received from the discovery of non-Euclidian geometries. Before Bolyai and Lobachevsky, geometry was, in the eyes of the philosophers, the paragon of perfect science; it was assumed that it provided unshakable certainty forever and for everybody. To proceed also in other branches of knowledge *more geometrico* was the great ideal of truth-seekers. All traditional epistemological concepts began to totter when the attempts to construct non-Euclidian geometries succeeded.

Yet praxeology is not geometry. It is the worst of all superstitions to assume that the epistemological characteristics of one branch of

knowledge must necessarily be applicable to any other branch. In dealing with the epistemology of the sciences of human action, one must
not take one's cue from geometry, mechanics, or any other science.

The assumptions of Euclid were once considered as self-evidently
true. Present-day epistemology looks upon them as freely chosen
postulates, the starting point of a hypothetical chain of reasoning.
Whatever this may mean, it has no reference at all to the problems of
praxeology.

The starting point of praxeology is a self-evident truth, the cognition
of action, that is, the cognition of the fact that there is such a thing as
consciously aiming at ends. There is no use cavilling about these words
by referring to philosophical problems that have no bearing upon our
problem. The truth of this cognition is as self-evident and as indispensable for the human mind as is the distinction between A and non-A.

5   The Reality of the External World

From the praxeological point of view it is not possible to question the
real existence of matter, of physical objects and of the external world.
Their reality is revealed by the fact that man is not omnipotent. There
is in the world something that offers resistance to the realization of his
wishes and desires. Any attempt to remove by a mere fiat what annoys
him and to substitute a state of affairs that suits him better for a state of
affairs that suits him less is vain. If he wants to succeed, he must proceed according to methods that are adjusted to the structure of something about which perception provides him with some information.
We may define the external world as the totality of all those things and
events that determine the feasibility or unfeasibility, the success or failure, of human action.

The much discussed question whether physical objects can or cannot be conceived as existing independently of the mind is vain. For
thousands of years the minds of physicians did not perceive germs and
did not divine their existence. But the success or failure of their endeavors to preserve their patients' health and lives depended on the way
germs influenced or did not influence the functioning of the patients'
bodily organs. The germs were real because they conditioned the outcome of events either by interfering or by not interfering, either by being present in or by being absent from the field.

6   Causality and Teleology

Action is a category that the natural sciences do not take into account. The scientist acts in embarking upon his research work, but in the orbit of natural events of the external world which he explores there is no such thing as action. There is agitation, there is stimulus and response, and, whatever some philosophers may object, there is cause and effect. There is what appears to be an inexorable regularity in the concatenation and sequence of phenomena. There are constant relations between entities that enable the scientist to establish the process called measurement. But there is nothing that would suggest aiming at ends sought; there is no ascertainable purpose.

The natural sciences are causality research; the sciences of human action are teleological. In establishing this distinction between the two fields of human knowledge, we do not express any opinion concerning the question whether the course of all cosmic events is or is not ultimately determined by a superhuman being's design. The treatment of this great problem transcends the range of man's reason and is outside the domain of any human science. It is in the realm that metaphysics and theology claim for themselves.

The purpose to which the sciences of human action refer is not the plans and ways of God, but the ends sought by acting men in the pursuit of their own designs. The endeavors of the metaphysical discipline commonly called philosophy of history to reveal in the flux of historical events the hidden plans of God or of some mythical agency (as, for instance, in the scheme of Marx, the material productive forces) are not science.

In dealing with a definite historical fact, for instance with the first World War, the historian has to find out the ends sought by the various individuals and groups of individuals who were instrumental in organizing these campaigns or in fighting the aggressors. He has to examine the outcome resulting from the actions of all people involved and compare it with the preceding state of affairs as well as with the intentions of the actors. But it is not the historian's business to search after a "higher" or "deeper" sense that manifested itself in the events or was realized by them. Perhaps there is such a hidden "higher" or "deeper" purpose or significance in the succession of historical events. But for mortal man there is no way open to learn something about such "higher" or "deeper" meanings.

7   The Category of Action

All the elements of the theoretical sciences of human action are already implied in the category of action and have to be made explicit by expounding its contents. As among these elements of teleology is also the category of causality, the category of action is the fundamental category of epistemology, the starting point of any epistemological analysis.

The very category or concept of action comprehends the concepts of means and ends, of preferring and putting aside, viz., of valuing, of success and failure, of profit and loss, of costs. As no action could be devised and ventured upon without definite ideas about the relation of cause and effect, teleology presupposes causality.

Animals are forced to adjust themselves to the natural conditions of their environment; if they do not succeed in this process of adjustment, they are wiped out. Man is the only animal that is able — within definite limits — to adjust his environment purposively to suit him better.

We can think of the evolutionary process that transformed the non-human ancestors of mankind into human beings as a succession of small, gradual changes spread over millions of years. But we cannot think of a mind in which the category of action would have been present only in an incomplete form. There is nothing in between a being driven exclusively by instincts and physiological impulses and a being that chooses ends and the means for the attainment of these ends. We cannot think of an acting being that would not *in concreto* distinguish what is end and what is means, what is success and what is failure, what he likes more and what he likes less, what is his profit or his loss derived from the action and what his costs are. In grasping all these things, he may, of course, err in his judgments concerning the role various external events and materials play in the structure of his action.

A definite mode of behavior is an action only if these distinctions are present in the mind of the man concerned.

8   The Sciences of Human Action

The German language has developed a term that would have been expedient to denote the totality of the sciences dealing with human action as distinguished from the natural sciences, viz., the term *Geisteswissenschaften*. Unfortunately some authors have heavily loaded this term with metaphysical and mystical implications that detract from its usefulness. In English the term *pneumatology* (suggested by Bentham[2] as the opposite of *somatology*) would have served the purpose, but it was never accepted. The term *moral sciences* as employed by John Stuart Mill is unsatisfactory on account of its etymological affinity with the normative discipline of ethics. The term *humanities* is traditionally employed exclusively for the historical branches of the sciences of human action. Thus we are forced to employ the rather heavy term "sciences of human action."

2. Bentham, "Essay on Nomenclature and Classification," Appendix No. IV to *Chrestomathia* (*Works*, ed. Bowring [1838–1843], VIII, 84 and 88).

CHAPTER 1

The Human Mind

1   The Logical Structure of the Human Mind

On the earth man occupies a peculiar position that distinguishes him from and elevates him above all other entities constituting our planet. While all the other things, animate or inanimate, behave according to regular patterns, man alone seems to enjoy — within definite limits — a modicum of freedom. Man meditates about the conditions of his own self and of his environment, devises states of affairs that, as he believes, would suit him better than the existing states, and aims by purposive conduct at the substitution of a more desired state for a less desired that would prevail if he were not to interfere.

There is within the infinite expanse of what is called the universe or nature a small field in which man's conscious conduct can influence the course of events.

It is this fact that induces man to distinguish between an external world subject to inexorable and inextricable necessity and his human faculty of thinking, cognizing, and acting. Mind or reason is contrasted with matter, the will with self-acting impulses, instincts, and physiological processes. Fully aware of the fact that his own body is subject to the same forces that determine all other things and beings, man imputes his ability to think, to will and to act to an invisible and intangible factor he calls his mind.

There were in the early history of mankind attempts to ascribe such a faculty of thinking and purposively aiming at ends chosen to many or even to all nonhuman things. Later people discovered that it was vain to deal with nonhuman things as if they were endowed with something analogous to the human mind. Then the opposite tendency developed. People tried to reduce mental phenomena to the operation of factors that were not specifically human. The most radical expression of this doctrine was already implied in the famous dictum of John Locke according to which the mind is a sheet of white paper upon which the external world writes its own story.

A new epistemology of rationalism aimed at the refutation of this integral empiricism. Leibniz added to the doctrine that nothing is in the intellect that has not previously been in the senses the proviso: except the intellect itself. Kant, awakened by Hume from his "dogmatic slumbers," put the rationalistic doctrine upon a new basis. Experience, he taught, provides only the raw material out of which the mind forms what is called knowledge. All knowledge is conditioned by the categories that precede any data of experience both in time and in logic. The categories are a priori; they are the mental equipment of the individual that enables him to think and — we may add — to act. As all reasoning presupposes the a priori categories, it is vain to embark upon attempts to prove or to disprove them.

The empiricist reaction against apriorism centers around a misleading interpretation of the non-Euclidean geometries, the nineteenth century's most important contribution to mathematics. It stresses the arbitrary character of axioms and premises and the tautological character of deductive reasoning. Deduction, it teaches, cannot add anything to our knowledge of reality. It merely makes explicit what was already implicit in the premises. As these premises are merely products of the mind and not derived from experience, what is deduced from them cannot assert anything about the state of the universe. What logic, mathematics, and other aprioristic deductive theories bring forward are at best convenient or handy tools for scientific operations. It is one of the tasks incumbent upon the scientist to choose for his work out of the multiplicity of the various existing systems of logic, geometry, and algebra the system that is most convenient for his specific purpose.[1] The axioms from which a deductive system departs are arbitrarily selected. They do not tell us anything about reality. There is no such thing as first principles a priori given to the human mind.[2] Such is the doctrine of the famous "Vienna Circle" and of other contemporary schools of radical empiricism and logical positivism.

In order to examine this philosophy, let us refer to the conflict between the Euclidian geometry and the non-Euclidian geometries which

---

1. Cf. Louis Rougier, *Traité de la connaissance* (Paris, 1955), pp. 13 ff.
2. *Ibid.*, pp. 47 ff.

gave rise to these controversies. It is an undeniable fact that technological planning guided by the Euclidian system resulted in effects that had
to be expected according to the inferences derived from this system. The
buildings do not collapse, and the machines run in the expected way.
The practical engineer cannot deny that this geometry aided him in his
endeavors to divert events of the real external world from the course they
would have taken in the absence of his intervention and to direct them
towards goals that he wanted to attain. He must conclude that this geometry, although based upon definite a priori ideas, affirms something
about reality and nature. The pragmatist cannot help admitting that Euclidian geometry works in the same way in which all a posteriori knowledge provided by the experimental natural sciences works. Aside from
the fact that the arrangement of laboratory experiments already presupposes and implies the validity of the Euclidian scheme, we must not
forget that the fact that the George Washington bridge over the Hudson
River and many thousand other bridges render the services the con-
structors wanted to get confirms the practical truth not only of the applied teachings of physics, chemistry, and metallurgy, but no less of
those of the geometry of Euclid. This means that the axioms from which
Euclid starts tell us something about the external world that to our
mind must appear no less "true" than the teachings of the experimental
natural sciences.

The critics of apriorism refer to the fact that for the treatment of certain problems recourse to one of the non-Euclidian geometries appears
more convenient than recourse to the Euclidian system. The solid bodies and light rays of our environment, says Reichenbach, behave according to the laws of Euclid. But this, he adds, is merely "a fortunate empirical fact." Beyond the space of our environment the physical world
behaves according to other geometries.[3] There is no need to argue this
point. For these other geometries also start from a priori axioms, not from
experimental facts. What the panempiricists fail to explain is how a deductive theory, starting from allegedly arbitrary postulates, renders valuable, even indispensable, services in the endeavors to describe correctly
the conditions of the external world and to deal with them successfully.

The fortunate empirical fact to which Reichenbach refers is the
fact that the human mind has the ability to develop theories which,

---

3. Cf. Hans Reichenbach, *The Rise of Scientific Philosophy* (University of California Press, 1951),
   p. 137.

although a priori, are instrumental in the endeavors to construct any a posteriori system of knowledge. Although logic, mathematics, and praxeology are not derived from experience, they are not arbitrarily made, but imposed upon us by the world in which we live and act and which we want to study.[4] They are not empty, not meaningless, and not merely verbal. They are — for man — the most general laws of the universe, and without them no knowledge would be accessible to man.

The a priori categories are the endowment that enables man to attain all that is specifically human and distinguishes him from all other beings. Their analysis is analysis of the human condition, the role man plays in the universe. They are the force that enables man to create and to produce all that is called human civilization.

2   A Hypothesis about the Origin of the A Priori Categories

The concepts of natural selection and evolution make it possible to develop a hypothesis about the emergence of the logical structure of the human mind and the a priori.

Animals are driven by impulses and instincts. Natural selection eliminated those specimens and species which developed instincts that were a liability in the struggle for survival. Only those endowed with impulses serviceable to their preservation survived and could propagate their species.

We are not prevented from assuming that in the long way that led from the nonhuman ancestors of man to the emergence of the species Homo sapiens some groups of advanced anthropoids experimented, as it were, with categorial concepts different from those of Homo sapiens and tried to use them for the guidance of their conduct. But as such pseudo categories were not adjusted to the conditions of reality, behavior directed by a quasi reasoning based upon them was bound to fail and to spell disaster to those committed to it. Only those groups could survive whose members acted in accordance with the right categories, i.e., with those that were in conformity with reality and therefore — to use the concept of pragmatism — worked.[5]

4. Cf. Morris Cohen, *A Preface to Logic* (New York: Henry Holt & Co., 1944), pp. 44 and 92; Mises, *Human Action*, pp. 72–91.
5. Mises, *Human Action*, pp. 86 ff.

However, reference to this interpretation of the origin of the a priori categories does not entitle us to call them a precipitate of experience, of a prehuman and prelogical experience as it were.[6] We must not blot out the fundamental difference between finality and the absence of finality.

The Darwinian concept of natural selection tries to explain phylogenetic change without recourse to finality as a natural phenomenon. Natural selection is operative not only without any purposive interference on the part of external elements; it operates also without any intentional behavior on the part of the various specimens concerned.

Experience is a mental act on the part of thinking and acting men. It is impossible to assign to it any role in a purely natural chain of causation the characteristic mark of which is the absence of intentional behavior. It is logically impossible to compromise between design and the absence of design. Those primates who had the serviceable categories survived, not because, having had the experience that their categories were serviceable, they decided to cling to them. They survived because they did not resort to other categories that would have resulted in their own extirpation. In the same way in which the evolutionary process eliminated all other groups whose individuals, because of specific properties of their bodies, were not fit for life under the special conditions of their environment, it eliminated also those groups whose minds developed in a way that made their use for the guidance of conduct pernicious.

The a priori categories are not innate ideas. What the normal — healthy — child inherits from his parents are not any categories, ideas, or concepts, but the human mind that has the capacity to learn and to conceive ideas, the capacity to make its bearer behave as a human being, i.e., to act.

However we may think about this problem, one thing is certain. Since the a priori categories emanating from the logical structure of the human mind have enabled man to develop theories the practical application of which has aided him in his endeavors to hold his own in the struggle for survival and to attain various ends that he wanted to attain, these categories provide some information about the reality of the universe. They are not merely arbitrary assumptions without any informative value, not mere conventions that could as well be replaced by some other conventions. They are the necessary mental tool to arrange sense

6. As J. Benda, *La crise du rationalisme* (Paris, 1949), pp. 27 ff., suggests.

data in a systematic way, to transform them into facts of experience, then [to transform] these facts into bricks to build theories, and finally [to transform] the theories into technics to attain ends aimed at.

The animals too are equipped with senses; some of them are even capable of sensing stimuli that do not affect man's senses. What prevents them from taking advantage of what their senses convey to them in the way man does, is not an inferiority of their sense equipment, but the fact that they lack what is called the human mind with its logical structure, its a priori categories.

Theory as distinct from history is the search for constant relations between entities or, what means the same, for regularity in the succession of events. In establishing epistemology as a theory of knowledge, the philosopher implicitly assumes or asserts that there is in the intellectual effort of man something that remains unchanged, viz., the logical structure of the human mind.

If there were nothing permanent in the manifestations of the human mind, there could not be any theory of knowledge, but merely a historical account of the various attempts made by men to acquire knowledge. The condition of epistemology would resemble that of the various branches of history, e.g., what is called political science. In the same way in which political science merely records what has been done or has been suggested in its field in the past, but is at a loss to tell anything about invariant relations among the elements with which it deals, epistemology would have to restrict its work to the assemblage of historical data about the mental activities of the past.

In stressing the fact that the logical structure of the human mind is common to all specimens of the species Homo sapiens, we do not want to assert that this human mind as we know it is the only or the best possible mental tool that could be devised or that has ever been and will ever be called into existence. In epistemology, as well as in all other sciences, we are dealing neither with eternity nor with conditions in parts of the universe from which no sign reaches our orbit nor with what may possibly happen in future eons. Perhaps there are somewhere in the infinite universe beings whose minds outrank our minds to the same extent as our minds surpass those of the insects. Perhaps there will once somewhere live beings who will look upon us with the same condescension as we look upon amoebae. But scientific thinking cannot indulge in such imagery. It is bound to limit itself to what is accessible to the human mind as it is.

3   The A Priori

One does not annul the cognitive significance of the a priori by qualify-
ing it as tautological. A tautology must *ex definitione* be the tautology —
restatement — of something said already previously. If we qualify Euclidian geometry as a hierarchical system of tautologies, we may say:
The theorem of Pythagoras is tautological as it expresses merely something that is already implied in the definition of a right-angled triangle.

But the question is: How did we get the first — the basic — proposition
of which the second — the derived — proposition is merely a tautology?
In the case of the various geometries the answers given today are either
(a) by an arbitrary choice or (b) on account of its convenience or suitability. Such an answer cannot be given with regard to the category of
action.

Neither can we interpret our concept of action as a precipitate of experience. It makes sense to speak of experience in cases in which also
something different from what was experienced *in concreto* could have
possibly been expected before the experience. Experience tells us something we did not know before and could not learn but for having had the
experience. But the characteristic feature of a priori knowledge is that
we cannot think of the truth of its negation or of something that would
be at variance with it. What the a priori expresses is necessarily implied
in every proposition concerning the issue in question. It is implied in all
our thinking and acting.

If we qualify a concept or a proposition as a priori, we want to say:
first, that the negation of what it asserts is unthinkable for the human
mind and appears to it as nonsense; secondly, that this a priori concept
or proposition is necessarily implied in our mental approach to all the
problems concerned, i.e., in our thinking and acting concerning these
problems.

The a priori categories are the mental equipment by dint of which
man is able to think and to experience and thus to acquire knowledge.
Their truth or validity cannot be proved or refuted as can those of a posteriori propositions, because they are precisely the instrument that enables us to distinguish what is true or valid from what is not.

What we know is what the nature or structure of our senses and of
our mind makes comprehensible to us. We see reality, not as it "is" and
may appear to a perfect being, but only as the quality of our mind and

of our senses enables us to see it. Radical empiricism and positivism do not want to admit this. As they describe it, reality writes, as experience, its own story upon the white sheets of the human mind. They admit that our senses are imperfect and do not fully and faithfully reflect reality. But they do not examine the power of the mind to produce, out of the material provided by sensation, an undistorted representation of reality. In dealing with the a priori we are dealing with the mental tools that enable us to experience, to learn, to know, and to act. We are dealing with the mind's power, and this implies that we are dealing with the limits of its power.

We must never forget that our representation of the reality of the universe is conditioned by the structure of our mind as well as of our senses. We cannot preclude the hypothesis that there are features of reality that are hidden to our mental faculties but could be noticed by beings equipped with a more efficient mind and certainly by a perfect being. We must try to become aware of the characteristic features and limitations of our mind in order not to fall prey to the illusion of omniscience.

The positivistic conceit of some of the forerunners of modern positivism manifested itself most blatantly in the dictum: God is a mathematician. How can mortals, equipped with manifestly imperfect senses, claim for their mind the faculty of conceiving the universe in the same way in which the wholly perfect may conceive it? Man cannot analyze essential features of reality without the help provided by the tools of mathematics. But the perfect being?

After all, it is quite supererogatory to waste time upon controversies concerning the a priori. Nobody denies or could deny that no human reasoning and no human search for knowledge could dispense with what these a priori concepts, categories, and propositions tell us. No quibbling can in the least affect the fundamental role played by the category of action for all the problems of the science of man, for praxeology, for economics, and for history.

4   The A Priori Representation of Reality

No thinking and no acting would be possible to man if the universe were chaotic, i.e., if there were no regularity whatever in the succession and concatenation of events. In such a world of unlimited contingency nothing could be perceived but ceaseless kaleidoscopic change. There would be no possibility for man to expect anything. All experience would be merely historical, the record of what has happened in the past. No inference from past events to what might happen in the future would be permissible. Therefore man could not act. He could at best be a passive spectator and would not be able to make any arrangements for the future, be it only for the future of the impending instant. The first and basic achievement of thinking is the awareness of constant relations among the external phenomena that affect our senses. A bundle of events that are regularly related in a definite way to other events is called a specific thing and as such distinguished from other specific things. The starting point of experimental knowledge is the cognition that an A is uniformly followed by a B. The utilization of this knowledge either for the production of B or for the avoidance of the emergence of B is called action. The primary objective of action is either to bring about B or to prevent its happening.

Whatever philosophers may say about causality, the fact remains that no action could be performed by men not guided by it. Neither can we imagine a mind not aware of the nexus of cause and effect. In this sense we may speak of causality as a category or an a priori of thinking and acting.

To the man anxious to remove by purposive conduct some uneasiness felt, the question occurs: Where, how, and when would it be necessary to interfere in order to obtain a definite result? Cognizance of the relation between a cause and its effect is the first step toward man's orientation in the world and is the intellectual condition of any successful activity. All attempts to find a satisfactory logical, epistemological, or metaphysical foundation for the category of causality were doomed to fail. All we can say about causality is that it is a priori not only of human thought but also of human action.

Eminent philosophers have tried to elaborate a complete list of the a priori categories, the necessary conditions of experience and thought. One does not belittle these attempts at analysis and systematization if one realizes that any proposed solution leaves a broad margin for the individual thinker's discretion. There is only one point about which there cannot be any disagreement, viz., that they all can be reduced to the a priori insight into the regularity in the succession of all observable phenomena of the external world. In a universe lacking this regularity there could not be any thinking and nothing could be experienced. For experience is the awareness of identity or the absence of identity in what is perceived; it is the first step toward a classification of events. And the concept of classes would be empty and useless if there were no regularity.

If there were no regularity, it would be impossible to resort to classification and to construct a language. All words signify bundles of regularly connected acts of perception or regular relations among such bundles. This is valid also of the language of physics, which the positivists want to elevate to the rank of a universal language of science. In a world without regularity there would not be any possibility of formulating "protocol sentences."[7] But even if it could be done, such a "protocol language" could not be the starting point of a science of physics. It would merely express historical facts.

If there were no regularity, nothing could be learned from experience. In proclaiming experience as the main instrument of acquiring knowledge, empiricism implicitly acknowledges the principles of regularity and causality. When the empiricist refers to experience, the meaning is: as A was in the past followed by B, and as we assume that there prevails a regularity in the concatenation and succession of natural events, we expect that A will also in the future be followed by B. Therefore there is a fundamental difference between the meaning of experience in the field of natural events and in the field of human action.

5   Induction

Reasoning is necessarily always deductive. This was implicitly admitted by all the attempts to justify ampliative induction by demonstrating or proving its logical legitimacy, i.e., by providing a deductive interpretation of induction. The plight of empiricism consists precisely in its failure to explain satisfactorily how it is possible to infer from observed facts something concerning facts yet unobserved.

All human knowledge concerning the universe presupposes and rests upon the cognition of the regularity in the succession and concatenation of observable events. It would be vain to search for a rule if there were no regularity. Inductive inference is conclusion from premises that invariably include the fundamental proposition of regularity.

7. About the "protocol language," cf. Carnap, "Die physikalische Sprache als Universalsprache der Wissenschaft," *Erkenntnis*, II (1931), 432–465, and Carnap, "Über Protokollsätze," *Erkenntnis*, III (1932/33), 215–228.

The practical problem of ampliative induction must be clearly distinguished from its logical problem. For the men who embark upon inductive inference are faced with the problem of correct sampling. Did we or did we not, out of the innumerable characteristics of the individual case or cases observed, choose those which are relevant for the production of the effect in question? Serious shortcomings of endeavors to learn something about the state of reality, whether in the mundane search for truth in everyday life or in systematic scientific research, are due to mistakes in this choice. No scientist doubts that what is *correctly* observed in one case must also be observed in all other cases offering the same conditions. The aim of laboratory experiments is to observe the effects of a change in one factor only, all the other factors remaining unchanged. Success or failure of such experiments presupposes, of course, the control of all the conditions that enter into their arrangement. The conclusions derived from experimentation are not based upon the repetition of the same arrangement, but upon the assumption that what happened in one case must necessarily also happen in all other cases of the same type. It would be impossible to infer anything from one case or from an innumerable series of cases without this assumption, which implies the a priori category of regularity. Experience is always the experience of past events and could not teach us anything about future events if the category of regularity were merely a vain assumption.

The panphysicalists' probability approach to the problem of induction is an abortive attempt to deal with induction without reference to the category of regularity. If we do not take account of regularity, there is no reason whatever to infer from anything that happened in the past what will happen in the future. As soon as we try to dispense with the category of regularity, all scientific effort appears useless, and the search for knowledge about what is popularly called the laws of nature becomes meaningless and futile. What is natural science about if not about the regularity in the flux of events?

Yet the category of regularity is rejected by the champions of logical positivism. They pretend that modern physics has led to results incompatible with the doctrine of a universally prevailing regularity and has shown that what has been considered by the "school philosophy" as the manifestation of a necessary and inexorable regularity is merely the product of a great number of atomic occurrences. In the microscopic sphere there is, they say, no regularity whatever. What macroscopic physics used to consider as the outcome of the operation of a strict regularity is merely the result of a great number of purely accidental elementary processes. The laws of macroscopic physics are not strict laws, but actually statistical laws. It could happen that the events in the microscopic sphere produce in the macroscopic sphere events that are different from those described by the merely statistical laws of macroscopic physics, although, they admit, the probability of such an occurrence is very small. But, they contend, the cognition of this possibility demolishes the idea that there prevails in the universe a strict regularity in the succession and concatenation of all events. The categories of regularity and causality must be abandoned and replaced by the laws of probability.[8]

It is true that the physicists of our age are faced with behavior on the part of some entities that they cannot describe as the outcome of a discernible regularity. However, this is not the first time that science has been faced with such a problem. The human search for knowledge must always encounter something that it cannot trace back to something else of which it would appear as the necessary effect. There is always in science some ultimate given. For contemporary physics the behavior of the atoms appears as such an ultimate given. The physicists are today at a loss to reduce certain atomic processes to their causes. One does not detract from the marvelous achievements of physics by establishing the fact that this state of affairs is what is commonly called ignorance.

What makes it possible for the human mind to orient itself in the bewildering multiplicity of external stimuli that affect our senses, to acquire what is called knowledge, and to develop the natural sciences is the cognition of an inevitable regularity and uniformity prevailing in the succession and concatenation of such events. The criterion that induces us to distinguish various classes of things is the behavior of these things. If a thing in only one regard behaves (reacts to a definite stimulus) in a way different from the behavior of other things to which it is equal in all other respects, it must be assigned to a different class.

We may look upon the molecules and the atoms the behavior of which is at the bottom of the probabilistic doctrines either as original elements or as derivatives of the original elements of reality. It does not matter which of these alternatives we choose. For in any case their behavior is the outcome of their very nature. (To say it more correctly: It is their behavior that constitutes what we call their nature.) As we see it,

8. Cf. Reichenbach, *op. cit.*, pp. 157 ff.

there are different classes of these molecules and atoms. They are not uniform; what we call molecules and atoms are groups composed of various subgroups the members of each of which in some regards differ in their behavior from the members of the other subgroups. If the behavior of the members of the various subgroups were different from what it is or if the numerical distribution of subgroup membership were different, the joint effect produced by the behavior of all the members of the groups would be different too. This effect is determined by two factors: the specific behavior of the members of each subgroup and the size of subgroup membership.

If the proponents of the probabilistic doctrine of induction had acknowledged the fact that there are various subgroups of microscopic entities, they would have realized that the joint effect of the operation of these entities results in what the macroscopic doctrine calls a law admitting of no exception. They would have had to confess that we do not know today why the subgroups differ from one another in some regards and how, out of the interaction of the members of the various subgroups, the definite joint effect emerges in the macroscopic sphere. Instead of this procedure they arbitrarily ascribe to the individual molecules and atoms the faculty of choosing among various alternatives of behavior. Their doctrine does not essentially differ from primitive animism. Just as the primitives ascribed to the "soul" of the river the power to choose between quietly flowing in its customary bed or inundating the adjacent fields, so they believe that these microscopic entities are free to determine some characteristics of their behavior, e.g., the speed and the path of their movements. In their philosophy it is implied that these microscopic entities are acting beings just like men.

But even if we were to accept this interpretation, we must not forget that human action is entirely determined by the individuals' physiological equipment and by all the ideas that were working in their minds. As we do not have any reason to assume that these microscopic entities are endowed with a mind generating ideas, we must assume that what are called their choices necessarily correspond to their physical and chemical structure. The individual atom or molecule behaves in a definite environment and under definite conditions precisely as its structure enjoins it. The speed and the path of its movements and its reaction to any encounters with factors external to its own nature or structure are strictly determined by this nature or structure. If one does not accept this interpretation, one indulges in the absurd metaphysical assumption that these molecules and atoms are equipped with free will in the sense which the most radical and naive indeterminist doctrines ascribed to man.

Bertrand Russell tries to illustrate the problem by comparing the position of quantum mechanics with regard to the behavior of the atoms to that of a railroad with regard to the behavior of the people making use of its facilities. The booking-office clerk at Paddington can discover, if he chooses, what proportion of travellers from that station go to Birmingham, what proportion to Exeter, and so on, but he knows nothing of the individual reasons that lead to one choice in one case and another in another. But Russell has to admit that the cases are not *"wholly analogous"* because the clerk can in his nonprofessional moments find out things about human beings that they do not mention when they are taking tickets, while the physicist in observing atoms has no such advantage.[9]

It is characteristic of the reasoning of Russell that he exemplifies his case by referring to the mind of a subaltern clerk to whom the unvarying performance of a strictly limited number of simple operations is assigned. What such a man (whose work could be performed as well by a vending automaton) thinks about things that transcend the narrow sphere of his duties is without avail. To the promoters who took the initiative in advancing the project of the railroad, to the capitalists who invested in the company, and to the managers who administer its operations, the problems involved appear in a quite different light. They built and operate the road because they anticipate the fact that there are certain reasons that will induce a number of people to travel from one point of their route to another. They know the conditions that determine these people's behavior, they know also that these conditions are changing, and they are intent upon influencing the size and the direction of these changes in order to preserve and to increase their patronage and the enterprise's proceeds. Their conduct of business has nothing to do with a reliance upon the existence of a mythical "statistical law." It is guided by the insight that there is a latent demand for travel facilities on the part of such a number of people that it pays to satisfy it by the operation of a railroad. And they are fully aware of the fact that the quantity of service they are able to sell could be drastically reduced one day to such an extent that they would be forced to go out of business.

9. B. Russell, *Religion and Science* (London: Home University Library, 1936), pp. 152 ff.

Bertrand Russell and all other positivists referring to what they call "statistical laws" are committing a serious blunder in commenting upon human statistics, i.e., statistics dealing with facts of human action as distinguished from the facts of human physiology. They do not take into account the fact that all these statistical figures are continually changing, sometimes more, sometimes less rapidly. There is in human valuations and consequently in human actions no such regularity as in the field investigated by the natural sciences. Human behavior is guided by motives, and the historian dealing with the past as well as the businessman intent upon anticipating the future must try to "understand" this behavior.[10]

If the historians and the acting individuals were not able to apply this specific understanding of their fellow men's behavior, and if the natural sciences and the acting individuals were not in a position to grasp something about the regularity in the concatenation and succession of natural events, the universe would appear to them as an unintelligible chaos and they could not contrive any means for the attainment of any ends. There would not be any reasoning, any knowledge, or any science, and there would not be any purposive influencing of environmental conditions on the part of man.

The natural sciences are possible only because there prevails regularity in the succession of external events. Of course, there are limits to what man can learn about the structure of the universe. There are unobservables and there are relations about which science up to now has not provided an interpretation. But the awareness of these facts does not falsify the categories of regularity and causality.

6   The Paradox of Probability Empiricism

Empiricism proclaims that experience is the only source of human knowledge and rejects as a metaphysical prepossession the idea that all experience presupposes a priori categories. But starting from its empiricistic approach, it postulates the possibility of events that have never been experienced by any man. Thus, we are told, physics cannot exclude the possibility that "when you put an ice cube into a glass of water,

10. About the "understanding," see below, pp. 49 ff.

the water starts boiling and the ice cube gets as cold as the interior of a deep-freezing cabinet." [11]

However, this neoempiricism is far from being consistent in the application of its doctrine. If there is no regularity in nature, nothing justifies the distinction between various classes of things and events. If one calls some molecules oxygen and others nitrogen, one implies that each member of these classes behaves in a definite way different from the behavior of the members of other classes. If one assumes that the behavior of an individual molecule can deviate from the way in which other molecules behave, one must either assign it to a special class or one must assume that its deviation was induced by the intervention of something to which other members of its class had not been exposed. If one says that one cannot exclude the possibility "that some day the molecules of the air in our room, by pure chance, arrive at an ordered state such that the molecules of oxygen are assembled on one side of the room and those of nitrogen on the other," [12] one implies that there is nothing either in the nature of oxygen and nitrogen or in the environment in which they are dwelling that results in the way in which they are distributed in the air. One assumes that the behavior of the individual molecules in all other regards is determined by their constitution, but that they are "free" to choose the place of their dwelling. One assumes quite arbitrarily that one of the characteristics of the molecules, viz., their movement, is not determined, while all their other characteristics are determined. One implies that there is something in the nature of the molecules — one is tempted to say: in their "soul" — that gives them the faculty of "choosing" the path of their wanderings. One fails to realize that a complete description of the behavior of the molecules ought also to include their movements. It would have to deal with the process that makes the molecules of oxygen and nitrogen associate with one another in the way in which they do in the air.

If Reichenbach had lived as a contemporary of magicians and tribal medicine men, he would have argued: Some people are afflicted with a disease having definite symptoms that kills them; others remain healthy and alive. We do not know of any factor the presence of which would cause the suffering of those stricken and the absence of which

11. Cf. Reichenbach, *op. cit.*, p. 162.
12. *Ibid.*, p. 161.

would cause the immunity of others. It is obvious that these phenomena cannot be dealt with scientifically if you cling to the superstitious concept of causality. All that we can know about them is the "statistical law" that $x\%$ of the population were afflicted and the rest not.

7 Materialism

Determinism must be clearly distinguished from materialism. Materialism declares that the only factors producing change are those that are accessible to investigation by the methods of the natural sciences. It does not necessarily deny the fact that human ideas, judgments of value, and volitions are real too and can produce definite changes. But as far as it does not deny this, it asserts that these ideal factors are the inevitable result of external events that necessarily beget in the bodily structure of men definite reactions. It is only a deficiency of the present state of the natural sciences that prevents us from imputing all manifestations of the human mind to the material — physical, chemical, biological and physiological — events that have brought them about. A more perfect knowledge, they say, will show how the material factors have necessarily produced in the man Mohammed the Moslem religion, in the man Descartes co-ordinate geometry, and in the man Racine *Phaedra*.

It is useless to argue with the supporters of a doctrine that merely establishes a program without indicating how it could be put into effect. What can be done and must be done is to disclose how its harbingers contradict themselves and what consequences must result from its consistent application.

If the emergence of every idea is to be dealt with as one deals with the emergence of all other natural events, it is no longer permissible to distinguish between true and false propositions. Then the theorems of Descartes are neither better nor worse than the bungling of Peter, a dull candidate for a degree, in his examination paper. The material factors cannot err. They have produced in the man Descartes co-ordinate geometry and in the man Peter something that his teacher, not enlightened by the gospel of materialism, considers as nonsense. But what entitles this teacher to sit in judgment upon nature? Who are the materialist philosophers to condemn what the material factors have produced in the bodies of the "idealistic" philosophers?

It would be useless for the materialists to point to pragmatism's distinction between what works and what does not work. For this distinction introduces into the chain of reasoning a factor that is foreign to the natural sciences, viz., finality. A doctrine or proposition works if conduct directed by it brings about the end aimed at. But the choice of the end is determined by ideas, is in itself a mental fact. So is also the judgment whether or not the end chosen has been attained. For consistent materialism it is not possible to distinguish between purposive action and merely vegetative, plant-like living.

Materialists think that their doctrine merely eliminates the distinction between what is morally good and morally bad. They fail to see that it no less wipes out any difference between what is true and what is untrue and thus deprives all mental acts of any meaning. If there stands between the "real things" of the external world and the mental acts nothing that could be looked upon as essentially different from the operation of the forces described by the traditional natural sciences, then we must put up with these mental phenomena in the same way as we respond to natural events. For a doctrine asserting that thoughts are in the same relation to the brain in which gall is to the liver,[13] it is not more permissible to distinguish between true and untrue ideas than between true and untrue gall.

8   The Absurdity of Any Materialistic Philosophy

The insurmountable difficulties that any materialistic interpretation of reality encounters can be shown in an analysis of the most popular materialistic philosophy, Marxian dialectical materialism.

Of course, what is called dialectical materialism is not a genuine materialistic doctrine. In its context the factor that produces all changes in the ideological and social conditions of man's history is the "material productive forces." Neither Marx nor any of his followers defined this term. But from all the examples they provided one must infer that what they had in mind was the tools, machines, and other artifacts that men employ in their productive activities. Yet these instruments are in themselves not ultimate material things, but the products of a purposive mental process.[14] But Marxism is the only attempt to carry a materialistic or

13. Karl Vogt, *Köhlerglaube and Wissenschaft* (2nd ed.; Giessen, 1855), p. 32.
14. Cf. Mises, *Theory and History*, pp. 108 ff.

quasi-materialistic doctrine beyond the mere enunciation of a metaphysical principle and to deduce from it all other manifestations of the human mind. Thus, we must refer to it if we want to show the fundamental shortcoming of materialism.

As Marx sees it, the material productive forces bring forth — independently of the will of men — the "production relations," i.e., the social system of property laws, and their "ideological superstructure," i.e., the juridical, political, religious, artistic, or philosophical ideas.[15] In this scheme, action and volition are ascribed to the material productive forces. They want to attain a definite goal, viz., they want to be freed from fetters that are hindering their development. Men are mistaken when they believe that they themselves are thinking, resorting to judgments of value, and acting. In fact, the production relations, the necessary effect of the prevailing stage of the material productive forces, are determining their ideas, volitions, and actions. All historical changes are ultimately produced by the changes in the material productive forces, which — as Marx implicitly assumes — are independent of human influence. All human ideas are the adequate superstructure of the material productive forces. These forces aim ultimately at the establishment of socialism, a transformation that is bound to come "with the inexorability of a law of nature."

Now let us for the sake of argument admit that the material productive forces have a constitution such that they are continually trying to free themselves from fetters upon their development. But why must, out of these attempts, first capitalism and, at a later stage of their development, socialism emerge? Do these forces reflect upon their own problems and finally reach the conclusion that the existing property relations, from having been forms of their own (viz., the forces') development, have turned into fetters[16] and that therefore they no longer correspond (*"entsprechen"*) to the present stage of their (viz., the forces') development?[17] And do they, on the ground of this insight, resolve that these fetters have to "burst asunder," and do they then proceed to action that causes them to burst asunder? And do they determine what new production relations have to take the place of the burst ones?

The absurdity of ascribing such thinking and acting to the material productive forces is so blatant that Marx himself paid but little

15. Cf. Karl Marx, *Zur Kritik der politischen Oekonomie*, ed. Kautsky (Stuttgart, 1897), pp. x–xii.
16. Marx, *op. cit.*, p. xi.
17. Marx and Engels, *The Communist Manifesto*, I.

attention to his famous doctrine when later, in his main treatise, *Capital*, he made more specific his prognostication about the coming of socialism. Here he refers not merely to action on the part of the material productive forces. He speaks of the proletarian masses who, dissatisfied with the progressive impoverishment that capitalism allegedly brings upon them, aim at socialism, obviously because they consider it as a more satisfactory system.[18]

Every variety of materialistic or quasi-materialistic metaphysics must imply converting an inanimate factor into a quasi man and ascribing to it the power to think, to pass judgments of value, to choose ends, and to resort to means for the attainment of the ends chosen. It must shift the specifically human faculty of acting to a nonhuman entity that it implicitly endows with human intelligence and discernment. There is no way to eliminate from an analysis of the universe any reference to the mind. Those who try it merely substitute a phantom of their own invention for reality.

From the point of view of his professed materialism — and, for that matter, from the point of view of any materialistic doctrine — Marx did not have the right to reject as false any doctrines developed by those with whom he disagreed. His materialism would have enjoined upon him a kind of listless recognition of any opinion and a readiness to attach to every idea advanced by a human being the same value as to any other idea advanced by somebody else. To escape such a self-defeating conclusion, Marx took recourse to his scheme of philosophy of history. He pretended that, by dint of a special charisma, denied to other mortals, he had a revelation that told him what course history must necessarily and unavoidably take. History leads to socialism. The meaning of history, the purpose for which man has been created (it is not said, by whom) is to realize socialism. There is no need to pay any attention to the ideas of people whom this message did not reach or who stubbornly refuse to believe in it.

What epistemology has to learn from this state of affairs is this: Any doctrine that teaches that some "real" or "external" forces write their own story in the human mind and thus tries to reduce the human mind to an apparatus that transforms "reality" into ideas in the way in which the digestive organs assimilate food is at a loss to distinguish between

18. Marx, *Das Capital* (7th ed.; Hamburg, 1914), Vol. I, ch. xxiv, p. 728. For a critical analysis of this argumentation, *see* Mises, *Theory and History*, pp. 102 ff.

what is true and what is not. The only way it can avoid a radical skepticism that does not have any means of sifting truth from falsehood in ideas is by distinguishing between "good" men, i.e., those who are equipped with the faculty of judging in conformity with the mysterious superhuman power that directs all affairs of the universe, and "bad" men, who lack this faculty. It must consider as hopeless any attempts to change the opinions of the "bad" men by discursive reasoning and persuasion. The only means to bring to an end the conflict of antagonistic ideas is to exterminate the "bad" men, i.e., the carriers of ideas that are different from those of the "good" men. Thus, materialism ultimately engenders the same methods of dealing with dissent that tyrants used always and everywhere.

In establishing this fact epistemology provides a clue for the understanding of the history of our age.

CHAPTER 2

The Activistic Basis of Knowledge

1   Man and Action

The characteristic feature of man is action. Man aims at changing
some of the conditions of his environment in order to substitute a state
of affairs that suits him better for another state that suits him less. All
manifestations of life and behavior with regard to which man differs
from all other beings and things known to him are instances of action
and can be dealt with only from what we may call an activistic point of
view. The study of man, as far as it is not biology, begins and ends with
the study of human action.

Action is purposive conduct. It is not simply behavior, but behavior
begot by judgments of value, aiming at a definite end and guided by
ideas concerning the suitability or unsuitability of definite means. It is
impossible to deal with it without the categories of causality and finality. It is conscious behavior. It is choosing. It is volition; it is a display of
the will.

Action is sometimes viewed as the human variety of the struggle for
survival common to all living beings. However, the term "struggle for
survival" as applied to animals and plants is a metaphor. It would be a
mistake to infer anything from its use. In applying literally the term
struggle to animals and plants one would ascribe to them the power to
become aware of factors threatening their existence, the will to preserve their own integrity, the mental faculty of finding means for its
preservation.

Seen from an activist point of view, knowledge is a tool of action. Its
function is to advise man how to proceed in his endeavors to remove
uneasiness. At the higher stages of man's evolution from the conditions
of the Stone Age to those of the age of modern capitalism, uneasiness
is also felt by the mere prevalence of ignorance concerning the nature

and the meaning of all things, no matter whether knowledge about these fundamental things would be of practical use for any technological planning. To live in a universe with whose final and real structure one is not familiar creates in itself a feeling of anxiety. To remove this anguish and to give men certainty about the last things has been from the earliest days the solicitude of religion and metaphysics. Later the philosophy of the Enlightenment and its affiliated schools promised that the natural sciences would solve all the problems involved. At any rate, it is a fact that to brood over the origin and essence of things, man's nature and his role in the universe, is one of the concerns of many people. Seen from this angle, the pure search for knowledge, not motivated by the desire to improve the external conditions of life, is also action, i.e., an effort to attain a more desirable state of affairs.

Another question is whether the human mind is fitted for the full solution of the problems involved. It may be argued that the biological function of reason is to aid man in his struggle for survival and the removal of uneasiness. Any step beyond the limits drawn by this function, it is said, leads to fantastic metaphysical speculations which are liable neither to demonstration nor to refutation. Omniscience is forever denied to man. Every search for truth must, sooner or later, but inevitably, lead to an ultimate given.[1]

The category of action is the fundamental category of human knowledge. It implies all the categories of logic and the category of regularity and causality. It implies the category of time and that of value. It encompasses all the specific manifestations of human life as distinguished from the manifestations of man's physiological structure which he has in common with all other animals. In acting, the mind of the individual sees itself as different from its environment, the external world, and tries to study this environment in order to influence the course of the events happening in it.

2   Finality

What distinguishes the field of human action from the field of external events as investigated by the natural sciences is the category of finality. We do not know of any final causes operating in what we call nature.

---

1. See below, p. 54.

But we know that man aims at definite goals chosen. In the natural sciences we search after constant relations among various events. In dealing with human action we search after the ends the actor wants or wanted to attain and after the result that his action brought about or will bring about.

The clear distinction between a field of reality about which man cannot learn anything else than that it is characterized by a regularity in the concatenation and succession of events and a field in which purposeful striving after ends chosen takes place is an achievement of a long evolution. Man, himself an acting being, was first inclined to explain all events as the manifestation of the action of beings acting in a way that was essentially not different from his own. Animism ascribed to all things of the universe the faculty of action. When experience moved people to drop this belief, it was still assumed that God or nature acts in a way not different from the ways of human action. The emancipation from this anthropomorphism is one of the epistemological foundations of modern natural science.

Positivist philosophy, which nowadays styles itself also scientific philosophy, believes that this rejection of finalism by the natural sciences implies the refutation of all theological doctrines as well as that of the teachings of the sciences of human action. It pretends that the natural sciences can solve all the "riddles of the universe" and provide an allegedly scientific answer to all the questions that may trouble mankind.

However, the natural sciences did not contribute and cannot contribute anything to the clarification of those problems with which religion tries to cope. The repudiation of naive anthropomorphism that imagined a supreme being either as a dictator or as a watchmaker was an achievement of theology and of metaphysics. With regard to the doctrine that God is wholly other than man and that his essence and nature cannot be grasped by mortal man, the natural sciences and a philosophy derived from them have nothing to say. The transcendent is beyond the realm about which physics and physiology convey information. Logic can neither prove nor disprove the core of theological doctrines. All that science — apart from history — can do in this regard is to expose the fallacies of magic and fetishistic superstitions and practices.

In denying the autonomy of the sciences of human action and their category of final causes, positivism enounces a metaphysical postulate that it cannot substantiate with any of the findings of the experimental methods of the natural sciences. It is a gratuitous pastime to apply to the description of the behavior of man the same methods the natural sciences apply in dealing with the behavior of mice or of iron. The same external events produce in different men and in the same men at different times different reactions. The natural sciences are helpless in face of this "irregularity." Their methods can deal only with events that are governed by a regular pattern. Besides, they do not have any room for the concepts of meaning, of valuation, and of ends.

3   Valuation

Valuing is man's emotional reaction to the various states of his environment, both that of the external world and that of the physiological conditions of his own body. Man distinguishes between more and less desirable states, as the optimists may express it, or between greater and lesser evils, as the pessimists are prepared to say. He acts when he believes that action can result in substituting a more desirable state for a less desirable.

The failure of the attempts to apply the methods and the epistemological principles of the natural sciences to the problems of human action is caused by the fact that these sciences have no tool to deal with valuing. In the sphere of the phenomena they study there is no room for any purposive behavior. The physicist himself and his physical research are entities outside the orbit he investigates. Judgments of value cannot be perceived by the observational attitudes of the experimenter and cannot be described in the protocol sentences of the language of physics. Yet they are, also from the viewpoint of the natural sciences, real phenomena, as they are a necessary link in chains of events that produce definite physical phenomena.

The physicist may laugh today at the doctrine that interpreted certain phenomena as the effect of a *horror vacui* [Medieval Latin, "horror of a vacuum," a supposed attribute of nature]. But he fails to realize that the postulates of panphysicalism are no less ridiculous. If one eliminates any reference to judgments of value, it is impossible to say anything about the actions of man, i.e., about all the behavior that is not merely the consummation of physiological processes taking place in the human body.

4　　The Chimera of Unified Science

The aim of all brands of positivism is to silence the sciences of human action. For the sake of argument we may abstain from analyzing positivism's contributions to the epistemology of the natural sciences both with regard to their originality and to their soundness. Neither do we have to dwell too long upon the motives that incited the positivist authors' passionate attacks upon the "unscientific procedure" of economics and history. They are advocating definite political, economic and cultural reforms which, as they believe, will bring about the salvation of mankind and the establishment of eternal bliss. As they cannot refute the devastating criticism that their fantastic plans met on the part of the economists, they want to suppress the "dismal science."

The question whether the term "science" ought to be applied only to the natural sciences or also to praxeology and to history is merely linguistic and its solution differs with the usages of various languages. In English the term science for many people refers only to the natural sciences.[2] In German it is customary to speak of a *Geschichtswissenschaft* [science of history] and to call various branches of history *Wissenschaft*, such as *Literaturwissenschaft* [science of literature], *Sprachwissenschaft* [science of speech (or linguistics)], *Kunstwissenschaft* [science of art], *Kriegswissenschaft* [science of war]. One can dismiss the problem as merely verbal, an inane quibbling about words.

Auguste Comte postulated an empirical science of sociology which, modelled after the scheme of classical mechanics, should deal with the laws of society and social facts. The many hundreds and thousands of the adepts of Comte call themselves sociologists and the books they are publishing contributions to sociology. In fact, they deal with various hitherto more or less neglected chapters of history and by and large proceed according to the well-tried methods of historical and ethnological research. It is immaterial whether they mention in the title of their books

2. Says R. G. Collingwood (*The Idea of History* [Oxford, 1946], p. 249): "There is a slang usage, like that for which 'hall' means a music hall or 'pictures' moving pictures, according to which 'science' means natural science." But "in the tradition of European speech . . . continuing unbroken down to the present day, the word 'science' means any organized body of knowledge." About the French usage, *see* Lalande, *Vocabulaire technique et critique de la philosophie* (5th ed.: Paris, 1947), pp. 933–940.

the period and the geographical area with which they are dealing. Their "empirical" studies necessarily always refer to a definite epoch of history and describe phenomena that come into existence, change, and disappear in the flux of time. The methods of the natural sciences cannot be applied to human behavior because this behavior, apart from what qualifies it as human action and is studied by the a priori science of praxeology, lacks the peculiarity that characterizes events in the field of the natural sciences, viz., regularity.

There is no way either to confirm or to reject by discursive reasoning the metaphysical ideas that are at the bottom of the blatantly advertised program of "Unified Science" as expounded in the *International Encyclopedia of Unified Science*, the holy writ of logical positivism, panphysicalism, and intolerant empiricism. Paradoxically enough, these doctrines, which started from a radical rejection of history, ask us to look upon all events as part of the subject matter of a comprehensive cosmic history. What we know about natural events, e.g., the behavior of sodium and levers, may, as they say, be valid only for the period of cosmic aggregation in which we ourselves and earlier generations of scientists lived. There is no reason whatever to assign to chemical and mechanical statements "any kind of universality" instead of treating them as historical ones.[3] Seen from this point of view, the natural sciences turn into a chapter of cosmic history. There is no conflict between physicalism and cosmic history.

We must admit that we do not know anything about conditions in a period of cosmic history for which the statements of what we call in our period the natural sciences will no longer be valid. In speaking about science and knowledge we have in mind only the conditions that our living, thinking, and acting permit us to investigate. What is beyond the conditions of this — perhaps temporarily limited — state of affairs is for us an unknown and unknowable region. In that sector of the universe which is accessible to our searching mind there prevails a dualism in the succession and concatenation of events. There is, on the one hand, the field of external events, about which we can learn only that there prevail mutual constant relations among them, and there is the field of human action, about which we cannot learn anything without resorting to the category of finality. All attempts to disregard this dualism are

3. Otto Neurath, *Foundations of the Social Sciences* (*International Encyclopedia of Unified Science*, Vol. II, No. 1 [3rd impression; University of Chicago Press, 1952]), p. 9.

dictated by arbitrary metaphysical repossessions, bring forth merely nonsense, and are useless for practical action.

The difference that exists in our environment between the behavior of sodium and that of an author who in his writings refers to sodium cannot be wiped out by any reference to the possibility that there were once or will be in the future periods of cosmic history about the conditions of which we do not know anything. All our knowledge must take into account the fact that with regard to sodium we do not know anything about final causes directing its behavior, while we know that man, e.g., in writing an essay about sodium, aims at definite ends. The attempts of behaviorism (or "behavioristics")[4] to deal with human action according to the stimulus-response scheme have failed lamentably. It is impossible to describe any human action if one does not refer to the meaning the actor sees in the stimulus as well as in the end his response is aiming at.

We know also the end that impels the champions of all these fads that nowadays parade under the name of Unified Science. Their authors are driven by the dictatorial complex. They want to deal with their fellow men in the way an engineer deals with the materials out of which he builds houses, bridges, and machines. They want to substitute "social engineering" for the actions of their fellow citizens and their own unique all-comprehensive plan for the plans of all other people. They see themselves in the role of the dictator—the *duce*, the *Führer*, the production tsar—in whose hands all other specimens of mankind are merely pawns. If they refer to *society* as an acting agent, they mean themselves. If they say that conscious action of society is to be substituted for the prevailing anarchy of individualism, they mean their own consciousness alone and not that of anybody else.

5　The Two Branches of the Sciences of Human Action

There are two branches of the sciences of human action, praxeology on the one hand, history on the other hand.

Praxeology is a priori. It starts from the a priori category of action and develops out of it all that it contains. For practical reasons praxeology does not as a rule pay much attention to those problems that are of no

4. *Ibid.*, p. 17.

use for the study of the reality of man's action, but restricts its work to those problems that are necessary for the elucidation of what is going on in reality. Its intent is to deal with action taking place under conditions that acting man has to face. This does not alter the purely aprioristic character of praxeology. It merely circumscribes the field that the individual praxeologists customarily choose for their work. They refer to experience only in order to separate those problems that are of interest for the study of man as he really is and acts from other problems that offer a merely academic interest. The answer to the question whether or not definite theorems of praxeology apply to a definite problem of action depends on the establishment of the fact whether or not the special assumptions that characterize this theorem are of any value for the cognition of reality. To be sure, it does not depend on the answer to the question whether or not these assumptions correspond to the real state of affairs that the praxeologists want to investigate. The imaginary constructions that are the main — or, as some people would rather say, the only — mental tool of praxeology describe conditions that can never be present in the reality of action. Yet they are indispensable for conceiving what is going on in this reality. Even the most bigoted advocates of an empiricist interpretation of the methods of economics employ the imaginary construction of an evenly rotating economy (static equilibrium), although such a state of human affairs can never be realized.[5]

Following in the wake of Kant's analyses, philosophers raised the question: How can the human mind, by aprioristic thinking, deal with the reality of the external world? As far as praxeology is concerned, the answer is obvious. Both, a priori thinking and reasoning on the one hand and human action on the other, are manifestations of the human mind. The logical structure of the human mind creates the reality of action. Reason and action are congeneric and homogeneous, two aspects of the same phenomenon. In this sense we may apply to praxeology the dictum of Empedocles γνῶσις τοῦ ὁμοίου τῷ ὁμοίῳ ["knowledge of like is by like" *].

Some authors have raised the rather shallow question how a praxeologist would react to an experience contradicting theorems of his aprioristic doctrine. The answer is: in the same way in which a mathematician will react to the "experience" that there is no difference between two

5. Mises, *Human Action*, pp. 237 ff.
* The passage is actually from Aristotle, who is referring to Empedocles, in *Metaphysics* and *De Anima*. (Translation by Professor Patricia Curd of Purdue University.)

apples and seven apples or a logician to the "experience" that A and non-A are identical. Experience concerning human action presupposes the category of human action and all that derives from it. If one does not refer to the system of the praxeological a priori, one must not and cannot talk of action, but merely of events that are to be described in terms of the natural sciences. Awareness of the problems with which the sciences of human action are concerned is conditioned by familiarity with the a priori categories of praxeology. Incidentally, we may also remark that any experience in the field of human action is specifically historical experience, i.e., the experience of complex phenomena, which can never falsify any theorem in the way a laboratory experiment can do with regard to the statements of the natural sciences.

Up to now the only part of praxeology that has been developed into a scientific system is economics. A Polish philosopher, Tadeusz Kotarbiński, is trying to develop a new branch of praxeology, the praxeological theory of conflict and war as opposed to the theory of cooperation or economics.[6]

The other branch of the sciences of human action is history. It comprehends the totality of what is experienced about human action. It is the methodically arranged record of human action, the description of the phenomena as they happened, viz., in the past. What distinguishes the descriptions of history from those of the natural sciences is that they are not interpreted in the light of the category of regularity. When the physicist says: if A encounters B, C results, he wants, whatever philosophers may say, to assert that C will emerge whenever or wherever A will encounter B under analogous conditions. When the historian refers to the battle of Cannae, he knows that he is talking about the past and that this particular battle will never be fought again.

Experience is a uniform mental activity. There are not two different branches of experience, one resorted to in the natural sciences, the other in historical research. Every act of experience is a description of what happened in terms of the observer's logical and praxeological equipment and his knowledge of the natural sciences. It is the observer's attitude that interprets the experience by adding it to his own already

6. T. Kotarbiński, "Considérations sur la théorie générale de la lutte," Appendix to Z Zagadnien Ogólnej Teorii Walki (Warsaw, 1938), pp. 65–92; the same author, "Idée de la methodologie générale praxeologie," Travaux du IXe Congrès International de Philosophie (Paris, 1937), IV, 190–194. The theory of games has no reference whatever to the theory of action. Of course, playing a game is action, but so is smoking a cigarette or munching a sandwich. See below, pp. 89 ff.

previously accumulated store of experienced facts. What distinguishes the experience of the historian from that of the naturalist and the physicist is that he searches for the meaning that the event had or has for those who were either instrumental in bringing it about or were affected by its happening.

The natural sciences do not know anything about final causes. For praxeology finality is the fundamental category. But praxeology abstracts from the concrete content of the ends men are aiming at. It is history that deals with the concrete ends. For history the main question is: What was the meaning the actors attached to the situation in which they found themselves and what was the meaning of their reaction, and, finally, what was the result of these actions? The autonomy of history or, as we may say, of the various historical disciplines consists in their dedication to the study of meaning.

It is perhaps not superfluous to emphasize again and again that when historians say "meaning," they refer to the meaning individual men — the actors themselves and those affected by their actions or the historians — saw in the actions. History as such has nothing in common with the point of view of philosophies of history that pretend to know the meaning that God or a quasi-God — such as the material productive forces in the scheme of Marx — attaches to the various events.

6   The Logical Character of Praxeology

Praxeology is a priori. All its theorems are products of deductive reasoning that starts from the category of action. The questions whether the judgments of praxeology are to be called analytic or synthetic and whether or not its procedure is to be qualified as "merely" tautological are of verbal interest only.

What praxeology asserts with regard to human action in general is strictly valid without any exception for every action. There is action and there is the absence of action, but there is nothing in between. Every action is an attempt to exchange one state of affairs for another, and everything that praxeology affirms with regard to exchange refers strictly to it. In dealing with every action we encounter the fundamental concepts end and means, success or failure, profit or loss, costs. An exchange can be either direct or indirect, i.e., effected through the interposition of an intermediary stage. Whether a definite action was indirect exchange has to be determined by experience. But if it was indirect exchange, then all that praxeology says about indirect exchange in general strictly applies to it.

Every theorem of praxeology is deduced by logical reasoning from the category of action. It partakes of the apodictic certainty provided by logical reasoning that starts from an a priori category.

Into the chain of praxeological reasoning the praxeologist introduces certain assumptions concerning the conditions of the environment in which an action takes place. Then he tries to find out how these special conditions affect the result to which his reasoning must lead. The question whether or not the real conditions of the external world correspond to these assumptions is to be answered by experience. But if the answer is in the affirmative, all the conclusions drawn by logically correct praxeological reasoning strictly describe what is going on in reality.

7   The Logical Character of History

History in the broadest sense of the term is the totality of human experience. History is experience, and all experience is historical. History comprehends also all the experience of the natural sciences. What characterizes the natural sciences as such is the fact that they approach the material of experience with the category of a strict regularity in the succession of events. History in the narrower sense of the term, i.e., the totality of experience concerning human action, must not and does not refer to this category. This distinguishes it epistemologically from the natural sciences.

Experience is always experience of the past. There is no experience and no history of the future. It would be unnecessary to repeat this truism if it were not for the problem of business forecasting by statisticians, about which something will be said later.[7]

History is the record of human actions. It establishes the fact that men, inspired by definite ideas, made definite judgments of value, chose definite ends, and resorted to definite means in order to attain the ends chosen, and it deals furthermore with the outcome of their actions, the state of affairs the action brought about.

What distinguishes the sciences of human action from the natural sciences is not the events investigated, but the way they are looked

7. See below, p. 67.

upon. The same event appears different when seen in the light of history and when seen in the light of physics or biology. What interests the historian in a case of murder or in a fire is not what interests the physiologist or the chemist if they are not acting as experts for a court of law. To the historian the events of the external world that are studied by the natural sciences count only as far as they affect human action or are produced by it.

The ultimate given in history is called individuality. When the historian reaches the point beyond which he cannot go farther, he refers to individuality. He "explains" an event—the origin of an idea or the performance of an action—by tracing it back to the activity of one man or of a multitude of men. Here he faces the barrier that prevents the natural sciences from dealing with the actions of men, viz., our inability to learn how definite external events produce in the minds of men definite reactions, i.e., ideas and volitions.

Futile attempts have been made to trace back human action to factors that can be described by the methods of the natural sciences. Stressing the fact that the urge to preserve one's own life and to propagate one's own species is inwrought in every creature, hunger and sex were proclaimed as the foremost or even as the only springs of human action. However, one could not deny that there prevail considerable differences between the way in which these biological urges affect the behavior of man and that of nonhuman beings and that man, besides aiming at satisfying his animal impulses, is also intent upon attaining other ends that are specifically human and therefore usually styled higher ends. That the physiological structure of the human body—first of all the appetites of the belly and of the sex glands—affects the choices of acting man has never been forgotten by the historians. After all, man is an animal. But he is the acting animal; he chooses between conflicting ends. It is precisely this that is the theme both of praxeology and of history.

8 The Thymological Method

The environment in which man acts is shaped by natural events on the one hand and by human action on the other. The future for which he plans will be codetermined by the actions of people who are planning and acting like himself. If he wants to succeed, he must anticipate their conduct.

The uncertainty of the future is caused not only by uncertainty concerning the future actions of other people, but also by insufficient knowledge concerning many natural events that are important for action. Meteorology provides some information about the factors that determine atmospheric conditions; but this knowledge at best enables the expert to predict the weather with some likelihood for a few days, never for longer periods. There are other fields in which man's foresight is even more limited. All that man can do in dealing with such insufficiently known conditions is to use what the natural sciences give him, however scanty this may be.

Radically different from the methods applied in dealing with natural events are those resorted to by man in anticipating the conduct of his fellow men. Philosophy and science for a long time paid little attention to these methods. They were considered as unscientific and not worthy of notice on the part of serious thinkers. When philosophers began to deal with them, they called them psychological. But this term became inappropriate when the techniques of experimental psychology were developed and almost all that earlier generations had called psychology was either altogether rejected as unscientific or assigned to a class of pursuits contemptuously styled as "mere literature" or "literary psychology." The champions of experimental psychology were confident that one day their laboratory experiments would provide a scientific solution of all the problems about which, as they said, the traditional sciences of human behavior babbled in childish or metaphysical talk.

In fact, experimental psychology has nothing to say and never did say anything about the problems that people have in mind when they refer to psychology in regard to the actions of their fellow men. The primary and central problem of "literary psychology" is meaning, something that is beyond the pale of any natural science and any laboratory activities. While experimental psychology is a branch of the natural sciences, "literary psychology" deals with human action, viz., with the ideas, judgments of value, and volitions that determine action. As the term "literary psychology" is rather cumbersome and does not permit one to form a corresponding adjective, I have suggested substituting for it the term *thymology*.[8]

8. Mises, *Theory and History*, pp. 264 ff.

Thymology is a branch of history or, as Collingwood formulated it, it belongs in "the sphere of history."[9] It deals with the mental activities of men that determine their actions. It deals with the mental processes that result in a definite kind of behavior, with the reactions of the mind to the conditions of the individual's environment. It deals with something invisible and intangible that cannot be perceived by the methods of the natural sciences. But the natural sciences must admit that this factor must be considered as real also from their point of view, as it is a link in a chain of events that result in changes in the sphere the description of which they consider as the specific field of their studies.

In analyzing and demolishing the claims of Comte's positivism, a group of philosophers and historians known as the *südwestdeutsche Schule* [southwestern German school] elaborated the category of understanding (*Verstehen*) that had already in a less explicit sense been familiar to older authors. This specific understanding of the sciences of human action aims at establishing the facts that men attach a definite meaning to the state of their environment, that they value this state and, motivated by these judgments of value, resort to definite means in order to preserve or to attain a definite state of affairs different from that which would prevail if they abstained from any purposeful reaction. Understanding deals with judgments of value, with the choice of ends and of the means resorted to for the attainment of these ends, and with the valuation of the outcome of actions performed.

The methods of scientific inquiry are categorically not different from the procedures applied by everybody in his daily mundane comportment. They are merely more refined and as far as possible purified

9. When H. Taine in 1863 wrote, "L'histoire au fond est un problème de psychologie" (*Histoire de la litérature anglaise* [10th ed.; Paris, 1899], Vol. I, Introduction, p. xlv), he did not realize that the kind of psychology he had in mind was not the natural science called experimental psychology, but that kind of psychology we call thymology and that thymology is in itself a historical discipline, a *Geisteswissenschaft* in the terminology of W. Dilthey (*Einleitung in die Geisteswissenschaften* [Leipzig, 1883]). R. G. Collingwood (*The Idea of History* [Oxford, 1946], p. 221) distinguishes between "historical thought" that "studies mind as acting in certain determinate ways in certain determinate situations" and a problematic other way of studying mind, viz., by "investigating its general characteristics in abstraction from any particular situation or particular action." The latter would be "not history, but mental science, psychology, or the philosophy of mind." Such "a positive mental science as rising above the sphere of history, and establishing the permanent and unchanging laws of human nature," he points [out] (p. 224), is "possible only to a person who mistakes the transient conditions of a certain historical age for the permanent conditions of human life."

of inconsistencies and contradictions. Understanding is not a method of procedure peculiar only to historians. It is practiced by infants as soon as they outgrow the merely vegetative stage of their first days and weeks. There is no conscious response of man to any stimuli that is not directed by understanding.

Understanding presupposes and implies the logical structure of the human mind with all the a priori categories. The biogenetic law represents the ontogeny of the individual as an abbreviated recapitulation of the phylogeny of the species. In an analogous way one may describe changes in the intellectual structure. The child recapitulates in his postnatal development the history of mankind's intellectual evolution.[10] The suckling becomes thymologically human when it begins faintly to dawn in his mind that a desired end can be attained by a definite mode of conduct. The nonhuman animals never proceed beyond instinctive urges and conditioned reflexes.

The concept of understanding was first elaborated by philosophers and historians who wanted to refute the positivists' disparagement of the methods of history. This explains why it was originally dealt with only as the mental tool of the study of the past. But the services understanding renders to man in throwing light on the past are only a preliminary stage in the endeavors to anticipate what may happen in the future. Seen from the practical point of view, man appears to be interested in the past only in order to be able to provide for the future. The natural sciences deal with experience — which necessarily is always the record of what happened in the past — because the categories of regularity and causality render such studies useful for the guidance of technological action, which inevitably always aims at an arrangement of future conditions. The understanding of the past performs a similar service in making action as successful as possible. Understanding aims at anticipating future conditions as far as they depend on human ideas, valuations, and actions. There is, but for Robinson Crusoe before he met his man Friday, no action that could be planned or executed without paying full attention to what the actor's fellow men will do. Action implies understanding other men's reactions.

The anticipation of events in the sphere explored by the natural sciences is based upon the categories of regularity and causality. There

10. *Language, Thought and Culture*, ed. by Paul Henle (University of Michigan Press, 1958), p. 48. Of course, the analogy is not complete, as the immense majority stop in their cultural evolution long before they reach the thymological heights of their age.

are in some byroads bridges that would collapse if a truck loaded with ten tons passed over them. We do not expect that such a load would make the George Washington bridge tumble. We firmly trust in the categories that are the foundations of our physical and chemical knowledge.

In dealing with the reactions of our fellow men we cannot rely upon such a regularity. We assume that, by and large, the future conduct of people will, other things being equal, not deviate without special reason from their past conduct, because we assume that what determined their past conduct will also determine their future conduct. However different we may know ourselves to be from other people, we try to guess how they will react to changes in their environment. Out of what we know about a man's past behavior, we construct a scheme about what we call his character. We assume that this character will not change if no special reasons interfere, and, going a step farther, we even try to foretell how definite changes in conditions will affect his reactions. Compared with the seemingly absolute certainty provided by some of the natural sciences, these assumptions and all the conclusions derived from them appear as rather shaky; the positivists may ridicule them as unscientific. Yet they are the only available approach to the problems concerned and indispensable for any action to be accomplished in a social environment.

Understanding does not deal with the praxeological side of human action. It refers to value judgments and the choice of ends and of means on the part of our fellow men. It refers not to the field of praxeology and economics, but to the field of history. It is a thymological category. The concept of a human character is a thymological concept. Its concrete content in each instance is derived from historical experience.

No action can be planned and executed without understanding of the future. Even an action of an isolated individual is guided by definite assumptions about the actor's future value judgments and is so far determined by the actor's image of his own character.

The term "speculate" was originally employed to signify any kind of meditation and forming of an opinion. Today it is employed with an opprobrious connotation to disparage those men who, in the capitalistic market economy, excel in better anticipating the future reactions of their fellow men than the average man does. The rationale of this semantic usage is to be seen in the inability of short-sighted people to notice the uncertainty of the future. These people fail to realize that all production activities aim at satisfying the most urgent future wants and that today no certainty about future conditions is available. They are not aware of the fact that there is a qualitative problem in providing for the future. In all the writings of the socialist authors there is not the slightest allusion to be found to the fact that one of the main problems of the conduct of production activities is to anticipate the *future* demands of the consumers.[11]

Every action is a speculation, i.e., guided by a definite opinion concerning the uncertain conditions of the future. Even in short-run activities this uncertainty prevails. Nobody can know whether some unexpected fact will not render vain all that he has provided for the next day or the next hour.

11. Mises, *Theory and History*, pp. 140 ff.

CHAPTER 3

Necessity and Volition

1   The Infinite

Negation, the notion of the absence or nonexistence of something or of the denial of a proposition, is conceivable to the human mind. But the notion of an absolute negation of everything, the representation of an absolute nothing, is beyond man's comprehension. So is the notion of the emergence of something out of nothing, the notion of an absolute beginning. The Lord, teaches the Bible, created the world out of nothing; but God himself was there from eternity and will be there in eternity, without a beginning and without an end.

As the human mind sees it, everything that happens, happens to something that existed before. The emergence of something new is seen as the evolution — the coming to maturity — of something that was potentially already present in what existed before. The totality of the universe as it was yesterday included already potentially the totality of the universe as it is today. The universe is an all-comprehensive context of elements, a continuity stretching back and forward into infinity, an entity to which to ascribe either an origin or an end is beyond the mental capacity of man.

Everything that is, is such as it is and not something different, because what preceded it was of a definite shape and structure and not of a different shape and structure.

We do not know what a superhuman, wholly perfect mind would think about these issues. We are merely men equipped with a human mind and cannot even imagine the potency and capacity of such a more perfect mind, essentially different from our mental powers.

2   The Ultimate Given

It follows that scientific research will never succeed in providing a full answer to what is called the riddles of the universe. It can never show how out of an inconceivable nothing emerged all that is and how one day all that exists may again disappear and the "nothing" alone will remain.

Scientific research sooner or later, but inevitably, encounters something ultimately given that it cannot trace back to something else of which it would appear as the regular or necessary derivative. Scientific progress consists in pushing further back this ultimately given. But there will always remain something that — for the human mind thirsting after full knowledge — is, at the given stage of the history of science, the provisional stopping point. It was only the rejection of all philosophical and epistemological thinking by some brilliant but one-sided physicists of the last decades that interpreted as a refutation of determinism the fact that they were at a loss to trace back certain phenomena — that for them were an ultimately given — to some other phenomena. Perhaps it is true, although not likely, that contemporary physics has at some points reached a barrier beyond which no further expansion of knowledge is possible for man. But however this may be, there is in all the teachings of the natural sciences nothing that could in any way be considered as incompatible with determinism.

The natural sciences are entirely based upon experience. All they know and deal with is derived from experience. And experience could not teach anything if there were no regularity in the concatenation and succession of events.

But the philosophy of positivism tries to assert much more than can be learned from experience. It pretends to know that there is nothing in the universe that could not be investigated and fully clarified by the experimental methods of the natural sciences. But it is admitted by everybody that up to now these methods have not contributed anything to the explanation of the phenomena of life as distinguished from physico-chemical phenomena. And all the desperate efforts to reduce thinking and valuing to mechanical principles have failed.

It is by no means the aim of the preceding remarks to express any opinion about the nature and structure of life and of the mind. This essay is, as has been said in the first words of its preface, not a contribution to philosophy. We have to refer to these problems only in order to show that the treatment that positivism accords to them implies a theorem for which no experimental justification whatever can be provided, viz., the theorem that all observable phenomena are liable to a reduction to physical and chemical principles. Whence do the positivists derive this theorem? It would be certainly wrong to qualify it as an a priori assumption. A characteristic mark of an a priori category is that any different assumption with regard to the topic concerned appears to the human mind as unthinkable and self-contradictory. But this is certainly not the case with the positivist dogma we are dealing with. The ideas taught by certain religious and metaphysical systems are neither unthinkable nor self-contradictory. There is nothing in their logical structure that would force any reasonable man to reject them for the same reasons he would, e.g., have to reject the thesis that there is no difference and distinction between A and non-A.

The gulf that in epistemology separates the events in the field investigated by the natural sciences from those in the field of thinking and acting has not been made narrower by any of the findings and achievements of the natural sciences. All we know about the mutual relation and interdependence of these two realms of reality is metaphysics. The positivist doctrine that denies the legitimacy of any metaphysical doctrine is no less metaphysical than many other doctrines at variance with it. This means: What a man in the present state of mankind's civilization and knowledge says about such issues as the soul, the mind, believing, thinking, reasoning, and willing does not have the epistemological character of natural science and can in no way be considered as scientific knowledge.

An honest man, perfectly familiar with all the achievements of contemporary natural science, would have to admit freely and unreservedly that the natural sciences do not know what the mind is and how it works and that their methods of research are not fit to deal with the problems dealt with by the sciences of human action.

It would have been wise on the part of the champions of logical positivism to take to heart Wittgenstein's advice: "Whereof one cannot speak, thereof one must be silent." [1]

3   Statistics

Statistics is the description in numerical terms of experiences concerning phenomena not subject to regular uniformity. As far as there is

1. L. Wittgenstein, *Tractatus Logico-Philosophicus* (New York, 1922), pp. 188 ff.

discernible regularity in the succession of phenomena, no recourse to statistics is needed. The objective of vital statistics is not to establish the fact that all men are mortal, but to give information about the length of human life, a magnitude that is not uniform. Statistics is therefore a specific method of history.

Where there is regularity, statistics could not show anything else than that A is followed in all cases by P and in no case by something different from P. If statistics show that A is in $x\%$ of all cases followed by P and in $(100 - x)\%$ of all cases by Q, we must assume that a more perfect knowledge will have to split up A into two factors B and C of which the former is regularly followed by P and the latter by Q.

Statistics is one of the resources of historical research. There are in the field of human action certain occurrences and events characteristic features of which can be described in numerical terms. Thus, e.g., the impact of a definite doctrine upon the minds of people does not permit of any numerical expression. Its "quantity" can be ascertained only by the method of the specific understanding of the historical disciplines.[2] But the number of people who lost their lives in struggles to arrange, by means of wars, revolutions, and assassinations, social conditions in agreement with a definite doctrine can be precisely determined in figures if all the documentation required is available.

Statistics provides numerical information about historical facts, that is, about events that happened at a definite period of time to definite people in a definite area. It deals with the past and not with the future. Like any other past experience, it can occasionally render important services in planning for the future, but it does not say anything that is directly valid for the future.

There is no such thing as [a] statistical [law]. People resort to the methods of statistics precisely where they are not in a position to find regularity in the concatenation and succession of events. The most celebrated statistical achievement, mortality tables, does not show stability, but changes in the mortality rates of the population. The average length of human life changes in the course of history, even if no changes were to emerge in the natural environment, because many factors that affect it are the result of human action, e.g., violence, diet, medical and prophylactic measures, the supply of foodstuffs, and others.

2. See below, p. 66.

The concept of [a] "statistical law" originated when some authors, in dealing with human conduct, failed to realize why certain statistical data change only slowly and, in blind enthusiasm, hastily identified slowness of change with absence of change. Thus, they believed themselves to have discovered regularities — laws — in the conduct of people for which neither they themselves nor anybody else had any other explanation than the — as must be emphasized, baseless — assumption that statistics had demonstrated them.[3] From the shaky philosophy of these authors physicists borrowed the term "statistical law," but they gave to it a connotation that differs from that attached to it in the field of human action. It is not our task to deal with the meaning these physicists and later generations of physicists attached to this term or with the services statistics can render to experimental research and to technology.

The orbit of the natural sciences is the field in which the human mind is able to discover constant relations between various elements. What characterizes the field of the sciences of human action is the absence of constant relations apart from those dealt with by praxeology. In the former group of sciences there are laws (of nature) and measurement. In the latter there is no measurement and — apart from praxeology — no laws; there is only history, including statistics.

4   Free Will

Man is not, like the animals, an obsequious puppet of instincts and sensual impulses. Man has the power to suppress instinctive desires, he has a will of his own, he chooses between incompatible ends. In this sense he is a moral person; in this sense he is free.

However, it is not permissible to interpret this freedom as independence of the universe and its laws. Man too is an element of the universe, descended from the original x out of which everything developed. He has inherited from the infinite line of his progenitors the physiological equipment of his self; in his postnatal life he was exposed to a variety of physical and mental experiences. He is at any instant of his life — his earthly pilgrimage — a product of the whole history of the

---

3. About the most eminent instance of this doctrine, that of H. Th. Buckle, *see* Mises, *Theory and History*, pp. 84 ff.

universe. All his actions are the inevitable result of his individuality as shaped by all that preceded. An omniscient being may have correctly anticipated each of his choices. (However, we do not have to deal with the intricate theological problems that the concept of omniscience raises.)

Freedom of the will does not mean that the decisions that guide a man's action fall, as it were, from outside into the fabric of the universe and add to it something that had no relation to and was independent of the elements which had formed the universe before. Actions are directed by ideas, and ideas are products of the human mind, which is definitely a part of the universe and of which the power is strictly determined by the whole structure of the universe.

What the term "freedom of the will" refers to is the fact that the ideas that induce a man to make a decision (a choice) are, like all other ideas, not "produced" by external "facts," do not "mirror," the conditions of reality, and are not "uniquely determined" by any ascertainable external factor to which we could impute them in the way in which we impute in all other occurrences an effect to a definite cause. There is nothing else that could be said about a definite instance of a man's acting and choosing than to ascribe it to this man's individuality.

We do not know how, out of the encounter of a human individuality, i.e., a man as he has been formed by all he has inherited and by all he has experienced, and a new experience definite ideas result and determine the individual's conduct. We do not even have any surmise how such knowledge could be acquired. More than that, we realize that if such knowledge were attainable for men, and if, consequently, the formation of ideas and thereby the will could be manipulated in the way machines are operated by the engineer, human conditions would be essentially altered. There would yawn a wide gulf between those who manipulate other people's ideas and will and those whose ideas and will are manipulated by others.

It is precisely the lack of such knowledge that generates the fundamental difference between the natural sciences and the sciences of human action.

In referring to the free will we are pointing out that in the production of events something can be instrumental about which the natural sciences cannot convey any information, something that the natural sciences cannot even notice. Yet our impotence to ascertain an absolute beginning out of nothing forces us to assume that also this invisible and intangible something — the human mind — is an inherent part of the universe, a product of its whole history.[4]

The traditional treatment of the problem of free will refers to the actor's vacillation before the final resolution. At this stage the actor wavers between different courses of action each of which seems to have some merits and demerits that the others lack. In comparing their pros and cons he is intent upon finding the decision that conforms to his personality and to the specific conditions of the instant as he sees them and thus upon satisfying best all his concerns. This means that his individuality — the product of all that he has inherited at birth from his ancestors and of all that he himself has experienced up to the critical moment — determines the final resolution. If later he reviews his past, he is aware of the fact that his comportment in any situation was fully determined by the kind of man he was at the instant of the action. It is immaterial whether in retrospect he himself or an unaffected observer can clearly describe all the factors that were instrumental in forming the past decision.

Nobody is in a position to predict with the same assurance with which the natural sciences make predictions how he himself and other people will act in the future. There is no method that would enable us to learn about a human personality all that would be needed to make such prognostications with the degree of certainty technology attains in its predictions.

The way in which historians and biographers proceed in analyzing and explaining the actions of the men with whom they are dealing reflects a more correct view of the problems involved than voluminous sophisticated treatises of moral philosophy. The historian refers to the spiritual milieu and the past experiences of the actor, to his knowledge or ignorance of all the data that could influence his decision, to his state of health, and to many other factors that could have played a role. But then, even after full attention has been paid to all these matters, something remains that defies any attempts at further interpretation, viz., the personality or individuality of the actor. When all is said about the case, there is finally no other answer to the question why Caesar crossed the Rubicon than: because he was Caesar. We cannot eliminate in dealing with human action reference to the actor's personality.

Men are unequal; individuals differ from one another. They differ because their prenatal as well as their postnatal history is never identical.

4. About these problems, *see* Mises, *Theory and History*, pp. 76–93.

5   Inevitability

All that happens was, under the prevailing conditions, bound to happen. It happened because the forces operating on its production were more powerful than the counteracting forces. Its happening was, in this sense, inevitable.

Yet the historian who in retrospect speaks of inevitability is not indulging in a pleonasm. What he means is to qualify a definite event or array of events A as the moving force producing a second event B; the proviso: provided no sufficiently powerful counteracting factor appeared, is self-understood. If such a counterpoise was lacking, A was bound to result in B, and it is permissible to call the outcome B inevitable.

In forecasting future events, apart from the field covered by praxeological law, reference to inevitability is a meaningless flower of speech. It does not add anything to the conclusive force of a prediction. It merely attests the infatuation of its author. This is all that needs to be said with regard to the prophetic effusions of the various systems of philosophy of history.[5] The "inexorability of a law of nature" (*Notwendigkeit eines Naturprozesses*) which Marx claimed for his prophecy[6] is just a rhetorical trick.

The momentous changes occurring in the course of cosmic and human history are the composite effect of a multitude of events. Each of these contributing events is strictly determined by the factors that preceded and produced it and so is the part each of them plays in the production of the momentous change. But if and as far as the chains of causation upon which the occurrence of these various contributing events depends are independent of one another, a situation may result that has induced some historians and philosophers to exaggerate the role chance plays in the history of mankind. They fail to realize that events are to be graded according to their size from the point of view of the weight of their effects and of their cooperation in the production of the composite effect. If only one of the minor events is altered, the influence upon the total outcome will also only be small.

It is a rather unsatisfactory way to argue: If the police in Sarajevo* had been more efficient on June 28, 1914, the archduke would not have been

5. About philosophy of history, *see* Mises, *Theory and History*, pp. 159 ff.
6. Marx, *Das Capital*, Vol. I, ch. xxiv, point 7.
* Site of the June 28, 1914, assassination of Archduke Francis Ferdinand, heir apparent to the Austro-Hungarian monarchy, which led to the outbreak of the First World War.

murdered and the World War and all its disastrous consequences would have been avoided. What made — in the sense referred to above — the Great War inevitable was the irreconcilable conflicts among the various linguistic groups (nationalities) of the Habsburg Monarchy, on the one hand, and, on the other hand, the German endeavors to build a navy strong enough to defeat the British naval forces. The Russian revolution was bound to come, as the Tsarist system and its bureaucratic methods were passionately rejected by the immense majority of the population; the outbreak of the war did not accelerate its coming; it rather delayed it for a short time. The fiery nationalism and etatism of the European peoples could not but result in war. These were the factors that made the Great War and its consequences inevitable, no matter whether the Serbian nationalists succeeded or failed in their attempts to murder the heir to the Austrian throne.

Political, social, and economic affairs are the outcome of the co-operation of all people. Although there prevail considerable differences with regard to the importance of the various individuals' contributions, they are commensurable and by and large capable of being replaced by those of other individuals. An accident that eliminates the work of an individual, be he even a rather eminent one, diverts the course of events only slightly from the line they would have followed if it had not occurred.

Conditions are different in the field of the greatest intellectual and artistic performances. The feat of the genius is outside the regular flow of human affairs. The genius too is in many regards determined by the conditions of his environment. But what gives to his work its specific lustre is something that is unique and cannot be duplicated by anyone else. We know neither what combination of genes produces the innate potentialities of the genius nor what kind of environmental conditions are needed to bring them to fruition. If he succeeds in avoiding all the dangers that could harm him and his accomplishments, the better for mankind. If an accident annihilates him, all the people lose something irreplaceable.

If Dante, Shakespeare, or Beethoven had died in childhood, man-kind would miss what it owes to them. In this sense we may say that chance plays a role in human affairs. But to stress this fact does not in the least contradict the a priori category of determinism.

CHAPTER 4

Certainty and Uncertainty

1   The Problem of Quantitative Definiteness

Laboratory experiments and observation of external phenomena enable the natural sciences to proceed with measurement and the quantification of knowledge. Referring to this fact, one used to style these sciences as the exact sciences and to belittle the lack of exactitude in the sciences of human action.

Today nobody any longer denies that on account of the insufficiency of our senses measurement is never perfect and precise in the full sense of these terms. It is only more or less approximate. Besides, the Heisenberg principle shows that there are relations that man cannot measure at all. There is no such thing as quantitative exactitude in our description of natural phenomena. However, the approximations that measurement of physical and chemical objects can provide are by and large sufficient for practical purposes. The orbit of technology is an orbit of approximate remeasurement and approximate quantitative definiteness.

In the sphere of human action there are no constant relations between any factors. There is consequently no measurement and no quantification possible. All measurable magnitudes that the sciences of human action encounter are quantities of the environment in which man lives and acts. They are historical facts, e.g., facts of economic or of military history, and are to be clearly distinguished from the problems with which the theoretical science of action — praxeology and especially also its most developed part, economics — deals.

Deluded by the idea that the sciences of human action must ape the technique of the natural sciences, hosts of authors are intent upon a quantification of economics. They think that economics ought to imitate chemistry, which progressed from a qualitative to a quantitative state.[1] Their motto is the positivistic maxim: Science is measurement. Supported by rich funds, they are busy reprinting and rearranging statistical data provided by governments, by trade associations, and by corporations and other enterprises. They try to compute the arithmetical relations among various of these data and thus to determine what they call, by analogy with the natural sciences, correlations and functions. They fail to realize that in the field of human action statistics is always history and that the alleged "correlations" and "functions" do not describe anything else than what happened at a definite instant of time in a definite geographical area as the outcome of the actions of a definite number of people.[2] As a method of economic analysis econometrics is a childish play with figures that does not contribute anything to the elucidation of the problems of economic reality.

2   Certain Knowledge

Radical empiricism rejects the idea that certain knowledge concerning the conditions of the universe is accessible to the minds of mortal men. It considers the a priori categories of logic and mathematics as assumptions or conventions, freely chosen on account of their convenience for the attainment of the kind of knowledge that man is able to acquire. All that is inferred by deduction from these a priori categories is merely tautological and does not convey any information about the state of reality. Even if we were to accept the untenable dogma of regularity in the concatenation and succession of natural events, the fallibility and insufficiency of the human senses makes it impossible to ascribe certainty to any a posteriori knowledge. We, human beings as we are, must acquiesce in this state of affairs. How things "really" are or may appear when looked upon from the vista of a superhuman intelligence, essentially different from the human mind as it works in the present eon of cosmic history, is for us inscrutable.

However, this radical scepticism does not refer to praxeological knowledge. Praxeology too starts from an a priori category and proceeds

---

1. J. Schumpeter, *Das Wesen and der Hauptinhalt der theoretischen Nationalökonomie* (Leipzig, 1908), pp. 606 ff.; W. Mitchell, "Quantitative Analysis in Economic Theory," *American Economic Review*, XV, 1 ff.; G. Cassel, *On Quantitative Thinking in Economics* (Oxford, 1935); and a daily increasing flood of books and articles.
2. Mises, *Human Action*, pp. 347 ff.

by deductive reasoning. Yet the objections raised by scepticism against the conclusiveness of a priori categories and a priori reasoning do not apply to it. For, as must be emphasized again, the reality the elucidation and interpretation of which is the task of praxeology is congeneric with the logical structure of the human mind. The human mind generates both human thinking and human action. Human action and human thinking stem from the same source and are in this sense homogeneous. There is nothing in the structure of action that the human mind cannot fully explain. In this sense praxeology supplies certain knowledge.

Man as he exists on this planet in the present period of cosmic history may one day disappear. But as long as there are beings of the species Homo sapiens there will be human action of the categorial kind praxeology deals with. In this restricted sense praxeology provides exact knowledge of future conditions.

In the field of human action all quantitatively determined magnitudes refer only to history and do not convey any knowledge that would mean something beyond the specific historical constellation that generated them. All general knowledge, that is, all knowledge that is applicable not only to a definite constellation of the past but to all praxeologically identical constellations of the past as well as of the future, is deductive knowledge ultimately derived from the a priori category of action. It refers rigidly to any reality of action as it appeared in the past and will appear in the future. It conveys precise knowledge of real things.

3   The Uncertainty of the Future

According to an often quoted dictum of Auguste Comte, the objective of the — natural — sciences is to know in order to predict what will happen in the future. These predictions are, as far as they refer to the effects of human action, conditional. They say: If A, then B. But they do not tell anything about the emergence of A. If a man absorbs potassium cyanide, he will die. But whether he will swallow this poison or not is left undecided.

The predictions of praxeology are, within the range of their applicability, absolutely certain. But they do not tell us anything about the value judgments of the acting individuals and the way they will determine their actions. All we can know about these value judgments has the categorial character of the specific understanding of the historical sciences of human action. Whether our anticipations of — our own or other people's — future value judgments and of the means that will be resorted to for adjusting action to these value judgments will be correct or not cannot be known in advance.

This uncertainty of the future is one of the main marks of the human condition. It taints all manifestations of life and action.

Man is at the mercy of forces and powers beyond his control. He acts in order to avoid as much as possible what, as he thinks, will harm himself. But he can at best succeed only within a narrow margin. And he can never know beforehand to what extent his acting will attain the end sought and, if it attains it, whether this action will in retrospect appear — to himself or to the other people looking upon it — as the best choice among those that were open to him at the instant he embarked upon it.

Technology based on the achievements of the natural sciences aims at full control within a definite sphere, which, of course, comprehends only a fraction of the events that determine man's fate. Although the progress of the natural sciences tends to enlarge the sphere of such scientifically directed action, it will never cover more than a narrow margin of possible events. And even within this margin there can never be absolute certainty. The result aimed at can be thwarted by the invasion of forces not yet sufficiently known or beyond human control. Technological engineering does not eliminate the aleatory element of human existence; it merely restricts its field a little. There always remains an orbit that to the limited knowledge of man appears as an orbit of pure chance and marks life as a gamble. Man and his works are always exposed to the impact of unforeseen and uncontrollable events. He cannot help banking upon the good luck not to be hit by them. Even dull people cannot fail to realize that their well-being ultimately depends on the operation of forces beyond man's wisdom, knowledge, prevision, and provision. With regard to these forces all human planning is vain. This is what religion has in mind when it refers to the unfathomable decrees of Heaven and turns to prayer.

4   Quantification and Understanding
     in Acting and in History

Many data with which the mind is concerned either in retrospect or in planning for the future can be expressed in numerical terms. Other relevant magnitudes can only be put into words of a nonmathematical language. In regard to such magnitudes the specific understanding of the sciences of human action is a substitute, as it were, for the unfeasibility of measurement.

In this sense the historian as well as the acting man speaks of the relevance of different events and actions in regard to their production of other events and of definite states of affairs. In this sense they distinguish between more important and less important events and facts and between greater men and lesser men.

Misjudgments in this quasi-quantitative evaluation of reality are pernicious if they occur in planning actions. Speculations are bound to fail if based upon an illusory anticipation of future conditions. Even if they are "qualitatively" correct, i.e., if the conditions they have anticipated really appear, they may bring disaster if they are "quantitatively" wrong, i.e., if they have erred concerning the dimensions of the effects or concerning the timing of their appearance. It is this that makes the long-range speculations of statesmen and of businessmen especially hazardous.

5   The Precariousness of Forecasting in Human Affairs

In forecasting what may or will happen in the future, man can either be right or mistaken. But his anticipation of future events cannot influence the course of nature. Whatever man may expect, nature will go its own way unaffected by any human expectations, desires, wishes, and hopes.

It is different in the sphere in which human action can operate. Forecasting may prove mistaken if it induces men to proceed successfully in a way that is designed to avoid the happening of the forecast events. What impels people to listen to the opinions of soothsayers or to consult with them is frequently the desire to avoid the emergence of undesirable events that, according to these prophecies, the future has in store for them. If, on the other hand, what the oracle promised them agreed with their wishes, they could react to the prophecy in two ways. Trusting to the oracle, they could either become indolent and neglect doing what had to be done in order to bring about the end forecast. Or they could, full of confidence, double their effort to attain the goal desired. In all such cases the content of the prophecy had the power to divert the course of affairs from the lines that it would have pursued in the absence of an allegedly authoritative forecast.

We may illustrate the issue by referring to business forecasting. If people are told in May that the boom going on will continue for several months and will not end in a crash before December, they will try to sell as soon as possible, at any rate before December. Then the boom will come to an end before the day indicated by the prediction.

6   Economic Prediction and the Trend Doctrine

Economics can predict the effects to be expected from resorting to definite measures of economic policies. It can answer the question whether a definite policy is able to attain the ends aimed at and, if the answer is in the negative, what its real effects will be. But, of course, this prediction can be only "qualitative." It cannot be "quantitative" as there are no constant relations between the factors and effects concerned. The practical value of economics is to be seen in this neatly circumscribed power of predicting the outcome of definite measures.

Those rejecting the aprioristic science of economics on account of its apriorism, the adepts of the various schools of Historicism and Institutionalism, ought from the point of view of their own epistemological principles to be prevented from expressing any judgment about the future effects to be expected from any definite policy. They cannot even know what a definite measure, whenever resorted to, brought about in the past. For what happened was always the result of the joint operation of a multitude of factors. The measure in question was only one of many factors contributing to the emergence of the final outcome. But even if these scholars are bold enough to assert that a definite measure in the past resulted in a definite effect, they would not — from the point of view of their own principles — be justified in assuming that therefore the same effect will be attained in the future too. Consistent Historicism and Institutionalism would have to refrain from issuing any opinion about the — necessarily future — effects of any measure or policy. They would have to restrict their teachings to the treatment of economic history. (We may pass over the question how economic history could be dealt with without economic theory.)

However, the public's interest in the studies labeled as economic is entirely due to the expectation that one can learn something about the methods to be resorted to for the attainment of definite ends. The students attending the courses of the professors of "economics" as well as the governments appointing "economic" advisers are anxious to get information about the future, not about the past. But all that these experts can tell them, if they remain faithful to their own epistemological principles, refers to the past.

To comfort their customers — statesmen, businessmen, and students — these scholars have developed the trend doctrine. They assume that trends that prevailed in the recent past — inappropriately often dubbed *the present*—will also continue in the future. If they consider the trend as undesirable, they recommend measures to change it. If they consider it as desirable, they are inclined to declare it as inevitable and irresistible and do not take into account the fact that trends manifested in history can change, often or rather always did change, and may change even in the immediate future.

7   Decision-Making

There are fads and fashions in the treatment of scientific problems and in the terminology of the scientific language.

What praxeology calls choosing is nowadays, as far as it concerns the choice of means, called decision-making. The neologism is designed to divert attention from the fact that what matters is not simply to make a choice, but to make the best possible choice. This means: to proceed in such a way that no less urgently desired end should be satisfied if its satisfaction prevents the attainment of a more urgently desired end. In the production processes directed in the market economy by profit-seeking business this is accomplished as far as possible with the intellectual aid of economic calculation. In a self-sufficient, closed, socialist system, which cannot resort to any economic calculation, the making of decisions concerning means is mere gambling.

8   Confirmation and Refutability

In the natural sciences a theory can be maintained only if it is in agreement with experimentally established facts. This agreement was, up to a short time ago, considered as confirmation. Karl Popper, in 1935, in *Logik der Forschung*[3] pointed out that facts cannot confirm a theory; they can only refute it. Hence a more correct formulation has to declare: A theory cannot be maintained if it is refuted by the data of experience. In this way experience restricts the scientist's discretion in constructing theories. A hypothesis has to be dropped when experiments show that it is incompatible with the established facts of experience.

It is obvious that all this cannot refer in any way to the problems of the sciences of human action. There are in this orbit no such things as experimentally established facts. All experience in this field is, as must be repeated again and again, historical experience, that is, experience of complex phenomena. Such an experience can never produce something having the logical character of what the natural sciences call "facts of experience."

If one accepts the terminology of logical positivism and especially also that of Popper, a theory or hypothesis is "unscientific" if *in principle* it cannot be refuted by experience. Consequently, all a priori theories, including mathematics and praxeology, are "unscientific." This is merely a verbal quibble. No serious man wastes his time in discussing such a terminological question. Praxeology and economics will retain their paramount significance for human life and action however people may classify and describe them.

The popular prestige that the natural sciences enjoy in our civilization is, of course, not founded upon the merely negative condition that their theorems have not been refuted. There is, apart from the outcome of laboratory experiments, the fact that the machines and all other implements constructed in accordance with the teachings of science run in the way anticipated on the ground of these teachings. The electricity-driven motors and engines provide a confirmation of the theories of electricity upon which their production and operation were founded. Sitting in a room that is lighted by electric bulbs, equipped with a telephone, cooled by an electric fan, and cleaned by a vacuum cleaner, the philosopher as well as the layman cannot help admitting that there may be something more in the theories of electricity than that up to now they have not been refuted by an experiment.

3. Now also available in an English-language edition, *The Logic of Scientific Discovery* (New York, 1959).

9   The Examination of Praxeological Theorems

The epistemologist who starts his lucubrations from the analysis of the methods of the natural sciences and whom blinkers prevent from perceiving anything beyond this field tells us merely that the natural sciences are the natural sciences and that what is not natural science is not natural science. About the sciences of human action he does not know anything, and therefore all that he utters about them is of no consequence.

It is not a discovery made by these authors that the theories of praxeology cannot be refuted by experiments nor confirmed by their successful employment in the construction of various gadgets. These facts are precisely one aspect of our problem.

The positivist doctrine implies that nature and reality, in providing the sense data that the protocol sentences register, write their own story upon the white sheet of the human mind. The kind of experience to which they refer in speaking of verifiability and refutability is, as they think, something that does not depend in any way on the logical structure of the human mind. It provides a faithful image of reality. On the other hand, they suppose, reason is arbitrary and therefore liable to error and misinterpretation.

This doctrine not only fails to make allowance for the fallibility of our apprehension of sense objects; it does not realize that perception is more than just sensuous apprehension, that it is an intellectual act performed by the mind. In this regard both associationism and Gestalt psychology agree. There is no reason to ascribe to the operation the mind performs in the act of becoming aware of an external object a higher epistemological dignity than to the operation the mind performs in describing its own ways of procedure.

In fact, nothing is more certain for the human mind than what the category of human action brings into relief. There is no human being to whom the intent is foreign to substitute by appropriate conduct one state of affairs for another state of affairs that would prevail if he did not interfere. Only where there is action are there men.

What we know about our own actions and about those of other people is conditioned by our familiarity with the category of action that we owe to a process of self-examination and introspection as well as of understanding of other people's conduct. To question this insight is no less impossible than to question the fact that we are alive.

He who wants to attack a praxeological theorem has to trace it back, step by step, until he reaches a point in which, in the chain of reasoning that resulted in the theorem concerned, a logical error can be unmasked. But if this regressive process of deduction ends at the category of action without having discovered a vicious link in the chain of reasoning, the theorem is fully confirmed. Those positivists who reject such a theorem without having subjected it to this examination are no less foolish than those seventeenth-century astronomers were who refused to look through the telescope that would have shown them that Galileo was right and they were wrong.

CHAPTER 5

On Some Popular Errors Concerning the Scope and Method of Economics

1 The Research Fable

The popular ideas concerning the methods the economists employ or ought to employ in the pursuit of their studies are fashioned by the belief that the methods of the natural sciences are also adequate for the study of human action. This fable is supported by the usage that mistakes economic history for economics. A historian, whether he deals with what is called general history or with economic history, has to study and to analyze the available records. He must embark upon research. Although the research activities of a historian are epistemologically and methodologically different from those of a physicist or a biologist, there is no harm in employing for all of them the same appellation, viz., research. Research is not only time-consuming. It is also more or less expensive.

But economics is not history. Economics is a branch of praxeology, the aprioristic theory of human action. The economist does not base his theories upon historical research, but upon theoretical thinking like that of the logician or the mathematician. Although history is, like all other sciences, at the background of his studies, he does not learn directly from history. It is, on the contrary, economic history that needs to be interpreted with the aid of the theories developed by economics.

The reason is obvious, as has been pointed out already. The historian can never derive theorems about cause and effect from the analysis of the material available. Historical experience is not laboratory experience. It is experience of complex phenomena, of the outcome of the joint operation of various forces.

This shows why it is wrong to contend that "it is from observation that even deductive economics obtains its ultimate premises." [1] What we can

---

1. John Neville Keynes, *The Scope and Method of Political Economy* (London, 1891), p. 165.

"observe" is always only complex phenomena. What economic history, observation, or experience can tell us is facts like these: Over a definite period of the past the miner John in the coal mines of the X company in the village of Y earned p dollars for a working day of n hours. There is no way that would lead from the assemblage of such and similar data to any theory concerning the factors determining the height of wage rates.

There are plenty of institutions for alleged economic research. They collect various materials, comment in a more or less arbitrary way upon the events to which these materials refer, and are even bold enough to make, on the ground of this knowledge about the past, prognostications concerning the future course of business affairs. Considering forecasting the future as their main objective, they call the series of data collected "tools." Considering the elaboration of plans for governmental action as their most eminent pursuit, they aspire to the role of an "economic general staff" assisting the supreme commander of the nation's economic effort. Competing with the research institutes of the natural sciences for government and foundation grants, they call their offices "laboratories" and their methods "experimental." Their effort may be highly appreciated from some points of view. But it is not economics. It is economic history of the recent past.

2 The Study of Motives

Public opinion still labors under the failure of classical economics to come to grips with the problem of value. Unable to solve the apparent paradox of valuation, the classical economists could not trace the chain of market transactions back to the consumer, but were forced to start their reasoning from the actions of the businessman, for whom the valuations of the buyers are a given fact. The conduct of the businessman in his capacity as a merchant serving the public is pertinently described by the formula: Buy in the cheapest and sell in the dearest market. The second part of this formula refers to the conduct of the buyers whose valuations determine the height of the prices they are prepared to pay for the merchandise. But nothing is said about the process that sets up these valuations. They are looked upon as given data. If one accepts this oversimplified formula, it is certainly possible to distinguish between businesslike conduct (falsely termed economic or rational conduct) and conduct determined by other considerations than those of business (falsely termed uneconomic or irrational conduct). But this mode of classification does not make any sense if we apply it to the behavior of the consumer.

The harm done by such and similar attempts to make distinctions was that they removed economics from reality. The task of economics, as many epigones of the classical economists practiced it, was to deal not with events as they really happened, but only with forces that contributed in some not clearly defined manner to the emergence of what really happened. Economics did not actually aim at explaining the formation of market prices, but at the description of something that together with other factors played a certain, not clearly described role in this process. Virtually it did not deal with real living beings, but with a phantom, "economic man," a creature essentially different from real man.

The absurdity of this doctrine becomes manifest as soon as the question is raised in what this economic man differs from real man. He is considered as a perfect egoist, as omniscient, and as exclusively intent upon accumulating more and more wealth. But it does not make any difference for the determination of market prices whether an "egoistic" buyer buys because he wants himself to enjoy what he bought or whether an "altruistic" buyer buys for some other reasons, for instance in order to make a gift to a charitable institution. Neither does it make any difference on the market whether the consumer in buying is guided by opinions that an unaffected spectator considers as true or false. He buys because he believes that to acquire the merchandise in question will satisfy him better than keeping the money or spending it for something else. Whether or not he aims at accumulating wealth, he always aims at employing what he owns for those ends which, as he thinks, will satisfy him best.

There is only one motive that determines all the actions of all men, viz., to remove, directly or indirectly, as much as possible any uneasiness felt. In the pursuit of this aim men are affected with all the frailties and weaknesses of human existence. What determines the real course of events, the formation of prices and all other phenomena commonly called economic as well as all other events of human history, is the attitudes of these fallible men and the effects produced by their actions liable to error. The eminence of the approach of modern marginal utility economics consists in the fact that it pays full attention to this state of affairs. It does not deal with the actions of an ideal man, essentially different from real man, but with the choices of all those who participate in social cooperation under the division of labor.

Economics, say many of its critics, assumes that everybody behaves in all his actions in a perfectly "rational" way and aims exclusively at the highest possible gain like the speculators buying and selling on the stock exchange. But real man, they assert, is different. He aims also at other ends than material advantage that can be expressed in monetary terms.

There is a whole bundle of errors and misunderstandings in this popular reasoning. The man who operates on the stock exchange is driven in this activity by one intention only, to enlarge his own competence. But exactly the same intention animates the acquisitive activity of all other people. The farmer wants to sell his produce at the highest price he can obtain, and the wage earner is anxious to sell his effort at the highest price obtainable. The fact that in comparing the remuneration that is offered to him the seller of commodities or services takes into account not only what he gets in terms of money but also all other benefits involved is fully consonant with his behavior as characterized in this description.

The specific goals that people aim at in action are very different and continually change. But all acting is invariably induced by one motive only, viz., to substitute a state that suits the actor better for the state that would prevail in the absence of his action.

3   Theory and Practice

A popular opinion considers economics as the science of business transactions. It assumes that economics is in the same relationship to the activities of a businessman as is the discipline of technology taught at schools and expounded in books to the activities of mechanics, engineers, and artisans. The businessman is the doer of things about which the economist merely talks and writes. Hence a businessman has, in his capacity as a practician, a better founded and more realistic knowledge, inside information, about the problems of economics than the theorist who observes the affairs of trade from without. The best method the theorist can choose to learn something about real conditions is to listen to what the performers say.

However, economics is not specifically about business; it deals with all market phenomena and with all their aspects, not only with the activities of a businessman. The conduct of the consumer — i.e., of everybody — is no less a topic of economic studies than that of anybody else. The businessman is, in his capacity as a businessman, not more closely related to or involved in the process that produces market phenomena than anybody else. The position of the economist with regard to the object of his studies is not to be compared to that of the author of books on technology to the practical engineers and workmen but rather to that of the biologist to the living beings — including men — whose vital functions he tries to describe. Not people with the best eyesight are experts in ophthalmology, but ophthalmologists even if they are myopic.

It is a historical fact that some businessmen, foremost among them David Ricardo, made outstanding contributions to economic theory. But there were other eminent economists who were "mere" theorists. What is wrong with the discipline that is nowadays taught in most universities under the misleading label of economics is not that the teachers and the authors of the textbooks are either not businessmen or failed in their business enterprises. The fault is with their ignorance of economics and with their inability to think logically.

The economist — like the biologist and the psychologist — deals with matters that are present and operative in every man. This distinguishes his work from that of the ethnologist who wants to record the mores and habits of a primitive tribe. The economist need not displace himself; he can, in spite of all sneers, like the logician and the mathematician, accomplish his job in an armchair. What distinguishes him from other people is not the esoteric opportunity to deal with some special material not accessible to others, but the way he looks upon things and discovers in them aspects which other people fail to notice. It was this that Philip Wicksteed had in mind when he chose for his great treatise a motto from Goethe's *Faust*: Human life — everybody lives it, but only to a few is it known.

4   The Pitfalls of Hypostatization

The worst enemy of clear thinking is the propensity to hypostatize, i.e., to ascribe substance or real existence to mental constructs or concepts.

In the sciences of human action the most conspicuous instance of this fallacy is the way in which the term *society* is employed by various schools of pseudo science. There is no harm in employing the term to signify the cooperation of individuals united in endeavors to attain definite ends. It is a definite aspect of various individuals' actions that constitutes what is called society or the "great society." But society itself is neither a substance, nor a power, nor an acting being. Only individuals act. Some of the individuals' actions are directed by the intention to cooperate with others. Cooperation of individuals brings about a state of affairs which the concept of society describes. Society does not exist apart from the thoughts and actions of people. It does not have "interests" and does not aim at anything. The same is valid for all other collectives.

Hypostatization is not merely an epistemological fallacy and not only misleads the search for knowledge. In the so-called social sciences it more often than not serves definite political aspirations in claiming for the collective as such a higher dignity than for the individual or even ascribing real existence only to the collective and denying the existence of the individual, calling it a mere abstraction.

The collectivists themselves disagree with one another in the appreciation of the various collectivistic constructs. They claim a higher reality and moral dignity for one collective than for others or, in a more radical way, even deny both real existence and dignity to the collectivistic constructs of other people. Thus, nationalists consider the "nation" as the only true collective, to which alone all individuals they consider as conationals owe allegiance, and stigmatize all other collectives — e.g., the religious communities — as of minor rank. However, epistemology does not have to deal with the political controversies implied.

In denying perseity, i.e., independent existence of their own, to the collectives, one does not in the least deny the reality of the effects brought about by the cooperation of individuals. One merely establishes the fact that the collectives come into being by the thoughts and actions of individuals and that they disappear when the individuals adopt a different way of thinking and acting. The thoughts and actions of a definite individual are instrumental in the emergence not only of one, but of various collectives. Thus, e.g., the same individual's various attitudes may serve to constitute the collectives nation, religious community, political party, and so on. On the other hand, a man may, without discontinuing entirely his belonging to a definite collective, occasionally or even regularly in some of his actions proceed in a way that is incompatible with the preservation of his membership. Thus, e.g., it happened in the recent history of various nations that practicing Catholics cast their votes in favor of candidates who openly avowed their hostility to the political aspirations of the Church and spurned its dogmas as fables. In dealing with collectives, the historian must pay attention to the degree to which the various ideas of cooperation determine the thinking and the actions of their members. Thus, in dealing with the history of the Italian Risorgimento, he has to investigate to what extent and in what manner the idea of an Italian national state and to what extent and in what manner the idea of a secular papal state influenced the attitudes of the various individuals and groups whose conduct is the subject of his studies.

The political and ideological conditions of the Germany of his day induced Marx to employ, in the announcement of his program of nationalization of the means of production, the term "society" instead of the term "state" (*Staat*), which is the German equivalent of the English term "nation." The socialist propaganda endowed the term "society" and the adjective "social" with an aura of sanctity that is manifested by the quasi-religious esteem that what is called "social work," i.e., the management of the distribution of alms and similar activities, enjoys.

5   On the Rejection of Methodological Individualism

No sensible proposition concerning human action can be asserted without reference to what the acting individuals are aiming at and what they consider as success or failure, as profit or loss. If we study the actions of the individuals, we learn everything that can be learned about acting, as there are, as far as we can see, in the universe no other entities or beings that, dissatisfied with the state of affairs that would prevail in the absence of their interference, are intent upon improving conditions by action. In studying action, we become aware both of the powers of man and of the limits of his powers. Man lacks omnipotence and can never attain a state of full and lasting satisfaction. All he can do is to substitute, by resorting to appropriate means, a state of lesser dissatisfaction for a state of greater dissatisfaction.

In studying the actions of individuals, we learn also everything about the collectives and society. For the collective has no existence and reality but in the actions of individuals. It comes into existence by ideas that move individuals to behave as members of a definite group and goes out of existence when the persuasive power of these ideas subsides. The only way to a cognition of collectives is the analysis of the conduct of its members.

There is no need to add anything to what has already been said by praxeology and economics to justify methodological individualism and to reject the mythology of methodological collectivism.[2] Even the most fanatical advocates of collectivism deal with the actions of individuals while they pretend to deal with the actions of collectives. Statistics does not register events that are happening in or to collectives. It records what happens with individuals forming definite groups. The criterion that determines the constitution of these groups is definite characteristics of the individuals. The first thing that has to be established in speaking of a social entity is the clear definition of what logically justifies counting or not counting an individual as a member of this group.

This is valid also with regard to those groups that are seemingly constituted by "material facts and realities" and not by "mere" ideological factors, e.g., the groups of people descended from the same ancestry or those of people living in the same geographical area. It is neither "natural" nor "necessary" that the members of the same race or the inhabitants of the same country cooperate with one another more closely than with members of other races or inhabitants of other countries. The ideas of race solidarity and racial hatred are no less ideas than any other ideas, and only where they are accepted by the individuals do they result in corresponding action. Also the primitive tribe of savages is kept together as an acting unit — a society — by the fact that its members are imbued with the idea that loyalty to the clan is the right way or even the only way open to them to take care of themselves. It is true that this primitive ideology was not seriously contested for thousands of years. But the fact that an ideology dominates people's minds for a very long time does not alter its praxeological character. Other ideologies too enjoyed considerable longevity, e.g., the monarchical principle of government.

The rejection of methodological individualism implies the assumption that the behavior of men is directed by some mysterious forces that defy any analysis and description. For if one realizes that what sets action in motion is ideas, one cannot help admitting that these ideas originate

---

2. *See* especially Mises, *Human Action*, pp. 41–44 and 145–153, and *Theory and History*, pp. 250 ff.

in the minds of some individuals and are transmitted to other individuals. But then one has accepted the fundamental thesis of methodological individualism, viz., that it is the ideas held by individuals that determine their group allegiance, and a collective no longer appears as an entity acting of its own accord and on its own initiative.

All interhuman relations are the offshoot of ideas and the conduct of individuals directed by these ideas. The despot rules because his subjects chose rather to obey him than to resist him openly. The slaveholder is in a position to deal with his slaves as if they were chattels because the slaves are willy nilly prepared to yield to his pretensions. It is an ideological transformation that in our age weakens and threatens to dissolve entirely the authority of parents, teachers, and clergymen.

The meaning of philosophical individualism has been lamentably misinterpreted by the harbingers of collectivism. As they see it, the dilemma is whether the concerns — interests — of the individuals should rank before those of one of the — arbitrarily selected — collectives. However, the epistemological controversy between individualism and collectivism has no direct reference to this purely political issue. Individualism as a principle of the philosophical, praxeological, and historical analysis of human action means the establishment of the facts that all actions can be traced back to individuals and that no scientific method can succeed in determining how definite external events, liable to a description by the methods of the natural sciences, produce within the human mind definite ideas, value judgments, and volitions. In this sense the individual that cannot be dissolved into components is both the starting point and the ultimate given of all endeavors to deal with human action.

The collectivistic method is anthropomorphic, as it simply takes it for granted that all concepts of the action of individuals can be applied to those of the collectives. It does not see that all collectives are the product of a definite way in which individuals act; they are an offshoot of ideas determining the conduct of individuals.

6   The Approach of Macroeconomics

The authors who think that they have substituted, in the analysis of the market economy, a holistic or social or universalistic or institutional or macroeconomic approach for what they disdain as the spurious individualistic approach delude themselves and their public. For all reasoning concerning action must deal with valuation and with the striving after definite ends, as there is no action not oriented by final causes. It is possible to analyze conditions that would prevail within a socialist system in which only the supreme tsar determines all activities and all the other individuals efface their own personality and virtually convert themselves into mere tools in the hands of the tsar's actions. For the theory of integral socialism it may seem sufficient to consider the valuations and actions of the supreme tsar only. But if one deals with a system in which more than one man's striving after definite ends directs or affects actions, one cannot avoid tracing back the effects produced by action to the point beyond which no analysis of actions can proceed, i.e., to the value judgments of the individuals and the ends they are aiming at.

The macroeconomic approach looks upon an arbitrarily selected segment of the market economy (as a rule: upon one nation) as if it were an integrated unit. All that happens in this segment is actions of individuals and groups of individuals acting in concert. But macroeconomics proceeds as if all these individual actions were in fact the outcome of the mutual operation of one macroeconomic magnitude upon another such magnitude.

The distinction between macroeconomics and microeconomics is, as far as terminology is concerned, borrowed from modern physics' distinction between microscopic physics, which deals with systems on an atomic scale, and molar physics, which deals with systems on a scale appreciable to man's gross senses. It implies that ideally the microscopic laws alone are sufficient to cover the whole field of physics, the molar laws being merely a convenient adaptation of them to a special, but frequently occurring problem. Molar law appears as a condensed and bowdlerised version of microscopic law.[3] Thus the evolution that led from macroscopic physics to microscopic physics is seen as a progress from a less satisfactory to a more satisfactory method of dealing with the phenomena of reality.

What the authors who introduced the distinction between macroeconomics and microeconomics into the terminology dealing with economic problems have in mind is precisely the opposite. Their doctrine implies that microeconomics is an unsatisfactory way of studying

3. A. Eddington, *The Philosophy of Physical Science* (New York and Cambridge, 1939), pp. 28 ff.

the problems involved and that the substitution of macroeconomics for microeconomics amounts to the elimination of an unsatisfactory method by the adoption of a more satisfactory method.

The macroeconomist deceives himself if in his reasoning he employs money prices determined on the market by individual buyers and sellers. A consistent macroeconomic approach would have to shun any reference to prices and to money. The market economy is a social system in which individuals are acting. The valuations of individuals as manifested in the market prices determine the course of all production activities. If one wants to oppose to the reality of the market economy the image of a holistic system, one must abstain from any use of prices.

Let us exemplify one aspect of the fallacies of the macroeconomic method by an analysis of one of its most popular schemes, the so-called national income approach.

Income is a concept of the accounting methods of profit-seeking business. The businessman serves the consumers in order to make profit. He keeps accounts to find out whether or not this goal has been attained. He (and likewise also capitalists, investors, who are not themselves active in business, and, of course, also farmers and owners of all kinds of real estate) compares the money equivalent of all the goods dedicated to the enterprise at two different instants of time and thus learns what the result of his transactions in the period between these two instants was. Out of such a calculation emerge the concepts of profit or loss as contrasted with that of capital. If the owner of the outfit to which this accounting refers calls the profit made "income," what he means is: If I consume the whole of it, I do not reduce the capital invested in the enterprise.

The modern tax laws call "income" not only what the accountant considers as the profit made by a definite business unit and what the owner of this unit considers as the income derived from the operations of this unit, but also the net earnings of professional people and the salaries and wages of employees. Adding together for the whole of a nation what is income in the sense of accountancy and what is income merely in the sense of the tax laws, one gets the figure called "national income."

The illusiveness of this concept of national income is to be seen in its dependence on changes in the purchasing power of the monetary unit. The more inflation progresses, the higher rises the national income. Within an economic system in which there is no increase in the supply of money and fiduciary media, progressive accumulation of capital and the improvement of technological methods of production that it engenders would result in a progressive drop in prices or, what is the same, a rise in the purchasing power of the monetary unit. The amount of goods available for consumption would increase and the average standard of living would improve, but these changes would not be made visible in the figures of the national income statistics.

The concept of national income entirely obliterates the real conditions of production within a market economy. It implies the idea that it is not activities of individuals that bring about the improvement (or impairment) in the quantity of goods available, but something that is above and outside these activities. This mysterious something produces a quantity called "national income," and then a second process "distributes" this quantity among the various individuals. The political meaning of this method is obvious. One criticizes the "inequality" prevailing in the "distribution" of national income. One taboos the question what makes the national income rise or drop and implies that there is no inequality in the contributions and achievements of the individuals that are generating the total quantity of national income.

If one raises the question what factors make the national income rise, one has only one answer: the improvement in equipment, the tools and machines employed in production, on the one hand, and the improvement in the utilization of the available equipment for the best possible satisfaction of human wants, on the other hand. The former is the effect of saving and the accumulation of capital, the latter of technological skill and of entrepreneurial activities. If one calls an increase in national income (not produced by inflation) economic progress, one cannot avoid establishing the fact that economic progress is the fruit of the endeavors of the savers, of the inventors, and of the entrepreneurs. What an unbiased analysis of the national income would have to show is first of all the patent inequality in the contribution of various individuals to the emergence of the magnitude called national income. It would furthermore have to show how the increase in the per-head quota of capital employed and the perfection of technological and entrepreneurial activities benefit — by raising the marginal productivity of labor and thereby wage rates and by raising the prices paid for the utilization of natural resources — also those classes of individuals who themselves did not contribute to the improvement of conditions and the rise in "national income."

The "national income" approach is an abortive attempt to provide a justification for the Marxian idea that under capitalism goods are "socially" (*gesellschaftlich*) produced and then "appropriated" by individuals. It puts things upside down. In reality, the production processes are activities of individuals cooperating with one another. Each individual collaborator receives what his fellow men — competing with one another as buyers on the market — are prepared to pay for his contribution. For the sake of argument one may admit that, adding up the prices paid for every individual's contribution, one may call the resulting total national income. But it is a gratuitous pastime to conclude that this total has been produced by the "nation" and to bemoan — neglecting the inequality of the various individuals' contributions — the inequality in its alleged distribution.

There is no nonpolitical reason whatever to proceed with such a summing up of all incomes within a "nation" and not within a broader or a narrower collective. Why national income of the United States and not rather "state income" of the State of New York or "county income" of Westchester County or "municipal income" of the municipality of White Plains? All the arguments that can be advanced in favor of preferring the concept of "national income" of the United States against the income of any of these smaller territorial units can also be advanced in favor of preferring the continental income of all the parts of the American continent or even the "world income" as against the national income of the United States. It is merely political tendencies that make plausible the choice of the United States as the unit. Those responsible for this choice are critical of what they consider as the inequality of individual incomes within the United States — or within the territory of another sovereign nation — and aim at more equality of the incomes of the citizens of their own nation. They are neither in favor of a worldwide equalization of incomes nor of an equalization within the various states that form the United States or their administrative subdivisions. One may agree or disagree with their political aims. But one must not deny that the macroeconomic concept of national income is a mere political slogan devoid of any cognitive value.

7   Reality and Play

The natural conditions of their existence enjoined upon the nonhuman ancestors of man the necessity of mercilessly fighting one another unto death. Inwrought in the animal character of man is the impulse of aggression, the urge to annihilate all those who compete with him in the endeavors to snatch a sufficient share of the scarce means of subsistence that do not suffice for the survival of all those born. Only for the strong animal was there a chance to remain alive.

What distinguishes man from the brutes is the substitution of social cooperation for mortal enmity. The inborn instinct of aggression is suppressed lest it disintegrate the concerted effort to preserve life and to make it more satisfactory by catering to specifically human wants. Supposedly, to calm down the repressed but not fully extinguished urges toward violent action, war dances and games were resorted to. What was once bitterly serious was now sportingly duplicated as a pastime. The tournament looks like fighting, but it is only a pageant. All the moves of the players are strictly regulated by the rules of the game. Victory does not consist in the annihilation of the other party, but in the attainment of a situation that the rules declare to be success. Games are not reality, but merely play. They are civilized man's outlet for deeply ingrained instincts of enmity. When the game comes to an end, the victors and the defeated shake hands and return to the reality of their social life, which is cooperation and not fighting.

One could hardly misinterpret more fundamentally the essence of social cooperation and the economic effort of civilized mankind than by looking upon it as if it were a fight or the playful duplication of fighting, a game. In social cooperation everyone in serving his own interests serves the interests of his fellow men. Driven by the urge to improve his own conditions, he improves the conditions of other people. The baker does not hurt those for whom he bakes bread; he serves them. All people would be hurt if the baker stopped producing bread and the physician no longer attended to the sick. The shoemaker does not resort to "strategy" in order to defeat his customers by supplying them with shoes. Competition on the market must not be confused with the pitiless biological competition prevailing between animals and plants or with the wars still waged between — unfortunately not yet completely — civilized nations. Catallactic competition on the market aims at assigning to every individual that function in the social system in which he can render to all his fellow men the most valuable of the services he is able to perform.

There have always been people who were emotionally unfit to conceive the fundamental principle of cooperation under the system of the division of tasks. We may try to understand their frailty thymologically.

The purchase of any commodity curtails the buyer's power to acquire some other commodity that he also wishes to get, although, of course, he considers its procurement as less important than that of the good he actually buys. From this point of view he looks upon any purchase he makes as an obstacle preventing him from satisfying some other wants. If he did not buy A or if he had to spend less for A, he would have been able to acquire B. There is, for narrow-minded people, but one step to the inference that it is the seller of A who forces him to forgo B. He sees in the seller not the man who makes it possible for him to satisfy one of his wants, but the man who prevents him from satisfying some other wants. The cold weather induces him to buy fuel for his stove and curtails the funds he can spend for other things. But he blames neither the weather nor his longing for warmth; he lays the blame on the dealer in coal. This bad man, he thinks, profits from his embarrassment.

Such was the reasoning that led people to the conclusion that the source from which the businessman's profits stem is their fellow men's need and suffering. According to this reasoning, the doctor makes his living from the patient's sickness, not from curing it. Bakeries thrive on hunger, not because they provide the means to appease the hunger. No man can profit but at the expense of some other men; one man's gain is necessarily another man's loss. In an act of exchange only the seller gains, while the buyer comes off badly. Commerce benefits the sellers by harming the buyers. The advantage of foreign trade, says the Mercantilist doctrine, old and new, consists in exporting, not in the imports purchased by the exports.[4]

In the light of this fallacy the businessman's concern is to hurt the public. His skill is the strategy, as it were, the art of inflicting as much evil as possible on the enemy. The adversaries whose ruin he plots are his prospective customers as well as his competitors, those who like himself embark upon raids against the people. The most appropriate method to investigate scientifically business activities and the market process, it is said, is to analyze the behavior and strategy of people engaged in games.[5]

In a game there is a definite prize that falls to the victor. If the prize has been provided by a third party, the defeated party goes away empty-handed. If the prize is formed by contributions of the players, the

4. Mises, *Human Action*, pp. 660 ff.

5. J. v. Neumann and O. Morgenstern, *Theory of Games and Economic Behavior* (Princeton University Press, 1944); R. Duncan Luce and H. Raiffa, *Games and Decisions* (New York, 1957); and many other books and articles.

defeated forfeit their stake for the benefit of the victorious party. In a game there are winners and losers. But a business deal is always advantageous for both parties. If both the buyer and the seller were not to consider the transaction as the most advantageous action they could choose under the prevailing conditions, they would not enter into the deal.[6]

It is true that business as well as playing a game is rational behavior. But so are all other actions of man. The scientist in his investigations, the murderer in plotting his crime, the office-seeker in canvassing for votes, the judge in search of a just decision, the missionary in his attempts to convert a nonbeliever, the teacher instructing his pupils, all proceed rationally.

A game is a pastime, is a means to employ one's leisure time and to banish boredom. It involves costs and belongs to the sphere of consumption. But business is a means—the only means—to increase the quantity of goods available for preserving life and rendering it more agreeable. No game can, apart from the pleasure it gives to the players and to the spectators, contribute anything to the improvement of human conditions.[7] It is a mistake to equate games with the achievements of business activity.

Man's striving after an improvement of the conditions of his existence impels him to action. Action requires planning and the decision which of various plans is the most advantageous. But the characteristic feature of business is not that it enjoins upon man decision-making as such, but that it aims at improving the conditions of life. Games are merriment, sport, and fun; business is life and reality.

8   Misinterpretation of the Climate of Opinion

One does not explain a doctrine and actions engendered by it if one declares that it was generated by the spirit of the age or by the personal or geographical environment of the actors. In resorting to such interpretations one merely stresses the fact that a definite idea was in agreement with other ideas held at the same time and in the same milieu by other people. What is called the spirit of an age, of the members of a collective,

---

6. Mises, *Human Action*, pp. 661 ff.
7. Games arranged for the entertainment of spectators are not games proper, but show business.

or of a certain milieu is precisely the doctrines prevailing among the individuals concerned.

The ideas that change the intellectual climate of a given environment are those unheard of before. For these new ideas there is no other explanation than that there was a man from whose mind they originated.

A new idea is an answer provided by its author to the challenge of natural conditions or of ideas developed before by other people. Looking backward upon the history of ideas — and the actions engendered by them — the historian may discover a definite trend in their succession and may say that "logically" the earlier idea made the emergence of the later idea due. However, such hindsight philosophy lacks any rational justification. Its tendency to belittle the contributions of the genius — the hero of intellectual history — and to ascribe his work to the juncture of events makes sense only in the frame of a philosophy of history that pretends to know the hidden plan that God or a superhuman power (such as the material productive forces in the system of Marx) wants to accomplish by directing the actions of all men. From the point of view of such a philosophy all men are puppets bound to behave exactly in the ways the demiurge has assigned to them.

9   The Belief in the Omnipotence of Thought

A characteristic feature of present-day popular ideas concerning social cooperation is what Freud has called the belief in the omnipotence of human thought (*die Allmacht des Gedankens*).[8] This belief is, of course, (apart from psychopaths and neurotics) not maintained with regard to the sphere that is investigated by the natural sciences. But in the field of social events it is firmly established. It developed out of the doctrine that ascribes infallibility to majorities.

The essential point in the political doctrines of the Enlightenment was the substitution of representative government for royal despotism. In the constitutional conflict in Spain in which champions of parliamentary government were fighting against the absolutist aspirations of the Bourbon Ferdinand VII, the supporters of a constitutional regime were called Liberals and those of the King Serviles. Very soon the name Liberalism was adopted all over Europe.

8. Freud, *Totem und Tabu* (Vienna, 1913), pp. 79 ff.

Representative or parliamentary government (also called government by the people or democratic government) is government by officeholders designated by the majority of the people. Demagogues tried to justify it by ecstatic babble about the supernatural inspiration of majorities. However, it is a serious mistake to assume that the nineteenth-century liberals of Europe and America advocated it because they believed in the infallible wisdom, moral perfection, inherent justice, and other virtues of the common man and therefore of majorities. The liberals wanted to safeguard the smooth evolution of all people's prosperity and material as well as spiritual well-being. They wanted to do away with poverty and destitution. As a means to attain these ends they advocated institutions that would make for peaceful cooperation of all citizens within the various nations as well as for international peace. They looked upon wars, whether civil wars (revolutions) or foreign wars, as a disturbance of the steady progress of mankind to more satisfactory conditions. They realized very well that the market economy, the very basis of modern civilization, involves peaceful cooperation and bursts asunder when people, instead of exchanging commodities and services, are fighting one another.

On the other hand, the liberals understood very well the fact that the might of the rulers ultimately rests, not upon material force, but upon ideas. As David Hume has pointed out in his famous essay *On the First Principles of Government*, the rulers are always a minority of people. Their authority and power to command obedience on the part of the immense majority of those subject to them are derived from the opinion of the latter that they best serve their own interests by loyalty to their chiefs and compliance with their orders. If this opinion dwindles, the majority will sooner or later rise in rebellion. Revolution — civil war — will remove the unpopular system of government and the unpopular rulers and replace them by a system and by officeholders whom the majority consider as more favorable to the promotion of their own concerns. To avoid such violent disturbances of the peace and their pernicious consequences, to safeguard the peaceful operation of the economic system, the liberals advocate government by the representatives of the majority. This scheme makes peaceful change in the arrangement of public affairs possible. It makes recourse to arms and bloodshed unnecessary not only in domestic but no less in international relations. When every territory can by majority vote determine whether it should form an independent state or a part of a larger state, there will no longer be wars to conquer more provinces.[9]

In advocating rule by the majority of the people, the nineteenth-century liberals did not nurture any illusions about the intellectual and moral perfection of the many, of the majorities. They knew that all men are liable to error and that it could happen that the majority, deluded by faulty doctrines propagated by irresponsible demagogues, could embark upon policies that would result in disaster, even in the entire destruction of civilization. But they were no less aware of the fact that no thinkable method of government could prevent such a catastrophe. If the small minority of enlightened citizens who are able to conceive sound principles of political management do not succeed in winning the support of their fellow citizens and converting them to the endorsement of policies that bring and preserve prosperity, the cause of mankind and civilization is hopeless. There is no other means to safeguard a propitious development of human affairs than to make the masses of inferior people adopt the ideas of the elite. This has to be achieved by convincing them. It cannot be accomplished by a despotic regime that instead of enlightening the masses beats them into submission. In the long run the ideas of the majority, however detrimental they may be, will carry on. The future of mankind depends on the ability of the elite to influence public opinion in the right direction.

These liberals did not believe in the infallibility of any human being nor in the infallibility of majorities. Their optimism concerning the future was based upon the expectation that the intellectual elite will persuade the majority to approve of beneficial policies.

The history of the last hundred years has not fulfilled these hopes. Perhaps the transition from the despotism of kings and aristocracies came too suddenly. At any rate, it is a fact that the doctrine that ascribes intellectual and moral excellence to the common man and consequently infallibility to the majority became the fundamental dogma of "progressive" political propaganda. In its farther logical development it generated the belief that in the field of society's political and economic organization any scheme devised by the majority can work satisfactorily. People no longer ask whether interventionism or socialism can

---

9. The first condition for the establishment of perpetual peace is, of course, the general adoption of the principles of laissez-faire capitalism. About this problem, *see* Mises, *Human Action*, pp. 680 ff., and Mises, *Omnipotent Government* (New Haven: Yale University Press, 1944 [Spring Mills, Penn.: Libertarian Press, 1985]), pp. 89 ff.

bring about the effects that their advocates are expecting from them. The mere fact that the majority of the voters ask for them is considered as an irrefutable proof that they can work and will inevitably result in the benefits expected. No politician is any longer interested in the question whether a measure is fit to produce the ends aimed at. What alone counts for him is whether the majority of the voters favor or reject it.[10] Only very few people pay attention to what "mere theory" says about socialism and to the experience of the socialist "experiments" in Russia and in other countries. Almost all our contemporaries firmly believe that socialism will transform the earth into a paradise. One may call it wishful thinking or the belief in the omnipotence of thought.

Yet the criterion of truth is that it works even if nobody is prepared to acknowledge it.

10 The Concept of a Perfect System of Government

The "social engineer" is the reformer who is prepared to "liquidate" all those who do not fit into his plan for the arrangement of human affairs. Yet historians and sometimes even victims whom he puts to death are not averse to finding some extenuating circumstances for his massacres or planned massacres by pointing out that he was ultimately motivated by a noble ambition: he wanted to establish the perfect state of mankind. They assign to him a place in the long line of the designers of utopian schemes.

Now it is certainly folly to excuse in this way the mass murders of such sadistic gangsters as Stalin and Hitler. But there is no doubt that many of the most bloody "liquidators" were guided by the ideas that inspired from time immemorial the attempts of philosophers to meditate on a perfect constitution. Having once hatched out the design of such an ideal order, the author is in search of the man who would establish it by suppressing the opposition of all those who disagree. In this vein, Plato was anxious to find a tyrant who would use his power for the realization of the Platonic ideal state. The question whether other people would like or dislike what he himself had in store for them never occurred

10. Symptomatic of this mentality is the weight ascribed by politicians to the findings of public opinion polls.

to Plato. It was an understood thing for him that the king who turned philosopher or the philosopher who became king was alone entitled to act and that all other people had, without a will of their own, to submit to his orders. Seen from the point of view of the philosopher who is firmly convinced of his own infallibility, all dissenters appear merely as stubborn rebels resisting what will benefit them.

The experience provided by history, especially by that of the last two hundred years, has not shaken this belief in salvation by tyranny and the liquidation of dissenters. Many of our contemporaries are firmly convinced that what is needed to render all human affairs perfectly satisfactory is brutal suppression of all "bad" people, i.e., of those with whom they disagree. They dream of a perfect system of government that — as they think — would have already long since been realized if these "bad" men, guided by stupidity and selfishness, had not hindered its establishment.

A modern, allegedly scientific school of reformers rejects these violent measures and puts the blame for all that is found wanting in human conditions upon the alleged failure of what is called "political science." The natural sciences, they say, have advanced considerably in the last centuries, and technology provides us almost monthly with new instruments that render life more agreeable. But "political progress has been nil." The reason is that "political science stood still." [11] Political science ought to adopt the methods of the natural sciences; it should no longer waste its time in mere speculations, but should study the "facts." For, as in the natural sciences, the "facts are needed before the theory." [12]

One can hardly misconstrue more lamentably every aspect of human conditions. Restricting our criticism to the epistemological problems involved, we have to say: What is today called "political science" is that branch of history that deals with the history of political institutions and with the history of political thought as manifested in the writings of authors who disserted about political institutions and sketched plans for their alteration. It is history, and can as such, as has been pointed out above, never provide any "facts" in the sense in which this term is used in the experimental natural sciences. There is no need to urge the political scientists to assemble all facts from the remote past and from recent history, falsely labelled "present experience." [13] Actually they do all

11. C. Northcote Parkinson, *The Evolution of Political Thought* (Boston, 1958), p. 306.
12. *Ibid.*, p. 309.
13. *Ibid.*, p. 314.

that can be done in this regard. And it is nonsensical to tell them that conclusions derived from this material ought "to be tested by experiments."[14] It is supererogatory to repeat that the sciences of human action cannot make any experiments.

It would be preposterous to assert apodictically that science will never succeed in developing a praxeological aprioristic doctrine of political organization that would place a theoretical science by the side of the purely historical discipline of political science. All we can say today is that no living man knows how such a science could be constructed. But even if such a new branch of praxeology were to emerge one day, it would be of no use for the treatment of the problem philosophers and statesmen were and are anxious to solve.

That every human action has to be judged and is judged by its fruits or results is an old truism. It is a principle with regard to which the Gospels agree with the often badly misunderstood teachings of the utilitarian philosophy. But the crux is that people widely differ from one another in their appraisal of the results. What some consider as good or best is often passionately rejected by others as entirely bad. The utopians did not bother to tell us what arrangement of affairs of state would best satisfy their fellow citizens. They merely expounded what conditions of the rest of mankind would be most satisfactory to themselves. Neither to them nor to their adepts who tried to realize their schemes did it ever occur that there is a fundamental difference between these two things. The Soviet dictators and their retinue think that all is good in Russia as long as they themselves are satisfied.

But even if for the sake of argument we put aside this issue, we have to emphasize that the concept of the perfect system of government is fallacious and self-contradictory.

What elevates man above all other animals is the cognition that peaceful cooperation under the principle of the division of labor is a better method to preserve life and to remove felt uneasiness than indulging in pitiless biological competition for a share in the scarce means of subsistence provided by nature. Guided by this insight, man alone among all living beings consciously aims at substituting social cooperation for what philosophers have called the state of nature or *bellum omnium contra omnes* ["war of all against all"] or the law of the jungle. However, in order to preserve peace, it is, as human beings are, indispensable to be

14. *Ibid.*, p. 314.

ready to repel by violence any aggression, be it on the part of domestic gangsters or on the part of external foes. Thus, peaceful human cooperation, the prerequisite of prosperity and civilization, cannot exist without a social apparatus of coercion and compulsion, i.e., without a government. The evils of violence, robbery, and murder can be prevented only by an institution that itself, whenever needed, resorts to the very methods of acting for the prevention of which it is established. There emerges a distinction between illegal employment of violence and the legitimate recourse to it. In cognizance of this fact some people have called government an evil, although admitting that it is a necessary evil. However, what is required to attain an end sought and considered as beneficial is not an evil in the moral connotation of this term, but a means, the price to be paid for it. Yet the fact remains that actions that are deemed highly objectionable and criminal when perpetrated by "unauthorized" individuals are approved when committed by the "authorities."

Government as such is not only not an evil, but the most necessary and beneficial institution, as without it no lasting social cooperation and no civilization could be developed and preserved. It is a means to cope with an inherent imperfection of many, perhaps of the majority of all people. If all men were able to realize that the alternative to peaceful social cooperation is the renunciation of all that distinguishes Homo sapiens from the beasts of prey, and if all had the moral strength always to act accordingly, there would not be any need for the establishment of a social apparatus of coercion and oppression. Not the state is an evil, but the shortcomings of the human mind and character that imperatively require the operation of a police power. Government and state can never be perfect because they owe their *raison d'être* to the imperfection of man and can attain their end, the elimination of man's innate impulse to violence, only by recourse to violence, the very thing they are called upon to prevent.

It is a double-edged makeshift to entrust an individual or a group of individuals with the authority to resort to violence. The enticement implied is too tempting for a human being. The men who are to protect the community against violent aggression easily turn into the most dangerous aggressors. They transgress their mandate. They misuse their power for the oppression of those whom they were expected to defend against oppression. The main political problem is how to prevent the police power from becoming tyrannical. This is the meaning of all

the struggles for liberty. The essential characteristic of Western civilization that distinguishes it from the arrested and petrified civilizations of
the East was and is its concern for freedom from the state. The history
of the West, from the age of the Greek πόλις [city-state] down to the
present-day resistance to socialism, is essentially the history of the fight
for liberty against the encroachments of the officeholders.

A shallow-minded school of social philosophers, the anarchists, chose
to ignore the matter by suggesting a stateless organization of mankind.
They simply passed over the fact that men are not angels. They were too
dull to realize that in the short run an individual or a group of individuals can certainly further their own interests at the expense of their own
and all other peoples' long-run interests. A society that is not prepared
to thwart the attacks of such asocial and short-sighted aggressors is helpless and at the mercy of its least intelligent and most brutal members.
While Plato founded his utopia on the hope that a small group of perfectly wise and morally impeccable philosophers will be available for
the supreme conduct of affairs, anarchists implied that all men without
any exception will be endowed with perfect wisdom and moral impec-
cability. They failed to conceive that no system of social cooperation
can remove the dilemma between a man's or a group's interests in the
short run and those in the long run.

Man's atavistic propensity to beat into submission all other people
manifests itself clearly in the popularity enjoyed by the socialist scheme.
Socialism is totalitarian. The autocrat or the board of autocrats alone is
called upon to act. All other men will be deprived of any discretion to
choose and to aim at the ends chosen; opponents will be liquidated. In
approving of this plan, every socialist tacitly implies that the dictators,
those entrusted with production management and all government functions, will precisely comply with his own ideas about what is desirable
and what undesirable. In deifying the state — if he is an orthodox Marxian, he calls it society — and in assigning to it unlimited power, he deifies
himself and aims at the violent suppression of all those with whom he
disagrees. The socialist does not see any problem in the conduct of
political affairs because he cares only for his own satisfaction and does
not take into account the possibility that a socialist government would
proceed in a way he does not like.

The "political scientists" are free from the illusions and self-deception
that mar the judgment of anarchists and socialists. But busy with the
study of the immense historical material, they become preoccupied

with detail, with the numberless instances of petty jealousy, envy, personal ambition, and covetousness displayed by the actors on the political scene. They ascribe the failure of all political systems heretofore tried to the moral and intellectual weakness of man. As they see it, these systems failed because their satisfactory functioning would have required men of moral and intellectual qualities only exceptionally present in reality. Starting from this doctrine, they tried to draft plans for a political order that could function automatically, as it were, and would not be embroiled by the ineptitude and vices of men. The ideal constitution ought to safeguard a blemishless conduct of public affairs in spite of the rulers' and the people's corruption and inefficiency. Those searching for such a legal system did not indulge in the illusions of the utopian authors who assumed that all men or at least a minority of superior men are blameless and efficient. They gloried in their realistic approach to the problem. But they never raised the question how men tainted by all the shortcomings inherent in the human character could be induced to submit voluntarily to an order that would prevent them from giving vent to their whims and fancies.

However, the main deficiency of this allegedly realistic approach to the problem is not this alone. It is to be seen in the illusion that government, an institution whose essential function is the employment of violence, could be operated according to the principles of morality that condemn peremptorily the recourse to violence. Government is beating into submission, imprisoning, and killing. People may be prone to forget it because the law-abiding citizen meekly submits to the orders of the authorities so as to avoid punishment. But the jurists are more realistic and call a law to which no sanction is attached an imperfect law. The authority of man-made law is entirely due to the weapons of the constables who enforce obedience to its provisions. Nothing of what is to be said about the necessity of governmental action and the benefits derived from it can remove or mitigate the suffering of those who are languishing in prisons. No reform can render perfectly satisfactory the operation of an institution the essential activity of which consists in inflicting pain.

Responsibility for the failure to discover a perfect system of government does not rest with the alleged backwardness of what is called political science. If men were perfect, there would not be any need for government. With imperfect men no system of government could function satisfactorily.

The eminence of man consists in his power to choose ends and to re-sort to means for the attainment of the ends chosen; the activities of gov-ernment aim at restricting this discretion of the individuals. Every man aims at avoiding what causes him pain; the activities of government ul-timately consist in the infliction of pain. All great achievements of man-kind were the product of a spontaneous effort on the part of individuals; government substitutes coercion for voluntary action. It is true, govern-ment is indispensable because men are not faultless. But designed to cope with some aspects of human imperfection, it can never be perfect.

11   The Behavioral Sciences

The self-styled behavioral sciences want to deal scientifically with hu-man behavior.[15] They reject as "unscientific" or "rationalistic" the meth-ods of praxeology and economics. On the other hand, they disparage his-tory as tainted with antiquarianism and devoid of any practical use for the improvement of human conditions. Their allegedly new discipline will, they promise, deal with every aspect of man's behavior and thereby provide knowledge that will render priceless services to the endeavors to improve the lot of mankind.

The representatives of these new sciences are not prepared to realize that they are historians and resorting to the methods of historical re-search.[16] What frequently—but not always—distinguishes them from the regular historians is that, like the sociologists, they choose as the subject matter of their investigations conditions of the recent past and aspects of human conduct that most historians of former times used to neglect. More remarkable may be the fact that their treatises often sug-gest a definite policy, as allegedly "taught" by history, an attitude which most of the sound historians have abandoned long since. It is not our concern to criticize the methods applied in these books and articles nor to question the rather naive political pre-possessions occasionally displayed by their authors. What makes it advisable to pay attention to these behavioral studies is their neglect of one of the most important epistemological principles of history, the principle of relevance.

15. One must not confuse the "behavioral sciences" with behaviorism. About the latter, *see* Mises, *Human Action*, p. 26.
16. Of course, some of these scholars deal with problems of medicine and hygiene.

In the experimental research of the natural sciences everything that can be observed is relevant enough to be recorded. As, according to the a priori that is at the outset of all research in the natural sciences, whatever happens is bound to happen as the regular effect of what preceded it, every correctly observed and described event is a "fact" that has to be integrated into the theoretical body of doctrine. No account of an experience is without some bearing on the whole of knowledge. Consequently, every research project, if conscientiously and skillfully performed, is to be considered as a contribution to mankind's scientific effort.

In the historical sciences it is different. They deal with human actions: the value judgments that incited them, the serviceableness of the means that were chosen for their performance, and the results brought about by them. Each of these factors plays its own role in the succession of events. It is the main task of the historian to assign as correctly as possible to every factor the range of its effects. This quasi quantification, this determination of each factor's *relevance*, is one of the functions that the specific understanding of the historical sciences is called upon to perform.[17]

In the field of history (in the broadest sense of the term) there prevail considerable differences among the various topics that could be made the subject of research activities. It is insignificant and meaningless to determine in general terms "the behavior of man" as the program of a discipline's activities. Man aims at an infinite number of different goals and resorts to an infinite number of different means for their attainment. The historian (or, for that matter, the behavioral scientist) must choose a subject of relevance for the fate of mankind and therefore also for the enlargement of our knowledge. He must not waste his time in trifles. In choosing the theme of his book he classifies himself. One man writes the history of liberty, another man the history of a card game. One man writes the biography of Dante, another the biography of a fashionable hotel's headwaiter.[18]

As the great subjects of mankind's past have already been dealt with by the traditional historical sciences, what is left to the behavioral sciences is detailed studies about the pleasures, sorrows, and crimes of the common man. To collect recent material about these and similar matters no special knowledge or technique is required. Every college boy can

17. See above, p. 66.
18. Karl Schriftgiesser, *Oscar of the Waldorf* (New York, 1943), 248 pages.

immediately embark upon some project. There is an unlimited number of subjects for doctoral dissertations and more sizable treatises. Many of them deal with quite trivial themes, devoid of any value for the enrichment of our knowledge.

These so-called behavioral sciences badly need a thorough reorientation from the point of view of the relevance principle. It is possible to write a voluminous book about every subject. But the question is whether such a book deals with something that counts as relevant from the point of view of theory or of practice.

CHAPTER 6

Further Implications of the Neglect of Economic Thinking

1   The Zoological Approach to Human Problems

Naturalism plans to deal with the problems of human action in the way zoology deals with all other living beings. Behaviorism wants to obliterate what distinguishes human action from the behavior of animals. In these schemes there is no room left for the specific human quality, man's distinctive feature, viz., the conscious striving after ends chosen. They ignore the human mind. The concept of finality is foreign to them.

Zoologically seen, man is an animal. But there prevails a fundamental difference between the conditions of all other animals and those of man. Every living being is naturally the implacable enemy of every other living being, especially of all other members of his own species. For the means of subsistence are scarce. They do not permit all specimens to survive and to consummate their existence up to the point at which their inborn vitality is fully spent. This irreconcilable conflict of essential interests prevails first of all among the members of the same species because they depend for their survival on the same foodstuffs. Nature is literally "red in tooth and claw."[1]

Man too is an animal. But he differs from all other animals as, by dint of his reason, he has discovered the great cosmic law of the higher productivity of cooperation under the principle of the division of labor. Man is, as Aristotle formulated it, the ζῷον πολιτικόν ["political animal"], the social animal, but he is "social" not on account of his animal nature, but on account of his specifically human quality. Specimens of

---

1. Tennyson, *In Memoriam*, LVI, iv.

his own zoological species are, for the human individual, not deadly enemies opposed to him in pitiless biological competition, but cooperators or potential cooperators in joint efforts to improve the external condition of his own welfare. An unbridgeable gulf separates man from all those beings that lack the ability to grasp the meaning of social cooperation.

2   The Approach of the "Social Sciences"

It is customary to hypostatize social cooperation by employing the term "society." Some mysterious superhuman agency, it is said, created society and peremptorily requires man to sacrifice the concerns of his petty egoism for the benefit of society.

The scientific treatment of the problems involved starts with the radical rejection of this mythological approach. What the individual forgoes in order to cooperate with other individuals is not his personal interests opposed to that of the phantom society. He forsakes an immediate boon in order to reap at a later date a greater boon. His sacrifice is provisional. He chooses between his interests in the short run and his interests in the long run, those which the classical economists used to call his "rightly understood" interests.

The utilitarian philosophy does not look upon the rules of morality as upon arbitrary laws imposed upon man by a tyrannical Deity with which man has to comply without asking any further questions. To behave in compliance with the rules that are required for the preservation of social cooperation is for man the only means to attain safely all those ends that he wants to attain.

The attempts to reject this rationalistic interpretation of morality from the point of view of Christian teachings are futile. According to the fundamental doctrine of Christian theology and philosophy, God has created the human mind in endowing man with his faculty of thinking. As both revelation and human reason are manifestations of the Lord's might, there cannot be ultimately any disagreement between them. God does not contradict himself. It is the object of philosophy and theology to demonstrate the concord between revelation and reason. Such was the problem the solution of which patristic and scholastic philosophy tried to achieve.[2] Most of these thinkers doubted

---

2. L. Rougier, *La scolastique et le Thomisme* (Paris, 1925), pp. 36 ff., 84 ff., 102 ff.

whether the human mind, unaided by revelation, would have been able to become aware of what the dogmas, especially those of the Incarnation and of the Trinity, taught. But they did not express serious doubts concerning the faculty of human reason in all other regards.

The popular attacks upon the social philosophy of the Enlightenment and the utilitarian doctrine as taught by the classical economists did not originate from Christian theology, but from theistic, atheistic, and antitheistic reasoning. They take for granted the existence of some collectives and ask neither how such collectives came into existence nor in what sense they "exist." They ascribe to the collective of their choice — mankind (*humanité*), race, nation (in the sense attached to this term in English and in French, which corresponds to the German *Staat*), nationality (the totality of all people speaking the same language), social class (in the Marxian sense), and some others — all the attributes of acting individuals. They maintain that the reality of these collectives can be perceived directly and that they exist apart from and above the actions of the individuals who belong to them. They assume that the moral law obliges the individual to subordinate his "petty" private desires and interests to those of the collective to which he belongs "by rights" and to which he owes unconditional allegiance. The individual who pursues his own interests or prefers loyalty to a "counterfeit" collective to that of the "true" collective is just a refractory.

The main characteristic of collectivism is that it does not take notice of the individual's will and moral self-determination. In the light of its philosophy the individual is born into a collective and it is "natural" and proper for him to behave as members of this collective are expected to behave. Expected by whom? Of course, by those individuals to whom, by the mysterious decrees of some mysterious agency, the task of determining the collective will and directing the actions of the collective has been entrusted.

In the *ancien régime* ["the old political and social order," commonly used to refer to the pre–French Revolution system] authoritarianism was based upon a kind of theocratic doctrine. The anointed king ruled by the grace of God; his mandate was from God. He was the personification of the realm. "France" was the name both of the king and of the country; the king's children were *enfants de France* ["children of France"]. Subjects who defied the royal orders were rebels.

The social philosophy of the Enlightenment rejected this presumption. It called all Frenchmen *enfants de la patrie* ["children of the homeland, or fatherland"], children of the fatherland. No longer was compulsory unanimity in all essential and political matters to be enforced. The institution of representative government — government by the people — acknowledges the fact that people may disagree with regard to political issues and that those sharing the same opinions consort with one another in parties. The party in office rules as long as it is supported by the majority.

The neoauthoritarianism of collectivism stigmatizes this "relativism" as contrary to human nature. The collective is seen as an entity above the concerns of the individuals. It is immaterial whether or not the individuals spontaneously agree with the concerns of the whole. At any rate it is their duty to agree. There are no parties; there is only the collective.[3] All the people are morally bound to comply with the collective's orders. If they disobey, they are forced to yield. This is what the Russian Marshal Zhukov called the "idealistic system" as opposed to the "materialistic system" of Western individualism that the commanding general of the American forces found "a little difficult" to defend.[4]

The "social sciences" are committed to the propagation of the collectivistic doctrine. They do not waste any words on the hopeless task of denying the existence of individuals or proving their villainy. In defining as the objective of the social sciences concern with "the activities of the individual as a member of a group"[5] and implying that the social sciences so defined cover everything that does not belong to the natural sciences, they simply ignore the existence of the individual. In their view, the existence of groups or collectives is an ultimate given. They do not attempt to search for the factors that make individuals

3. Etymologically, the term "party" is derived from the term "part" as contrasted with the term "whole." A brotherless party does not differ from the whole and is therefore not a party. The slogan "one-party system" was invented by the Russian Communists (and aped by their adepts, the Italian Fascists and the German Nazis) to conceal the abolition of the individual's freedom and right to dissent.

4. About this incident, see W. F. Buckley, Up from Liberalism (New York, 1959), pp. 164–168.

Editor's note: Buckley quoted from a July 1957 press conference of President Dwight D. Eisenhower's in which he described a discussion he had had with Marshal Zhukov, when he, Eisenhower, was the commander general of the U.S. forces. Eisenhower said he had known Marshal Zhukov and had "had a most satisfactory acquaintanceship and friendship with him. I think he was a confirmed Communist. . . . We tried each to explain to the other just what our systems meant, to the individual, and I was very hard put to it when he insisted that their system appealed to the idealistic, and we completely to the materialistic, and I had a very tough time trying to defend our position."

5. E. R. A. Seligman, "What Are the Social Sciences?" Encyclopedia of the Social Sciences, I, 3.

cooperate with one another and thus create what is called groups or collectives. For them the collective, like life or mind, is a primary phenomenon the origin of which science cannot trace back to the operation of some other phenomenon. Consequently, the social sciences are at a loss to explain how it can happen that there exists a multitude of collectives and that the same individuals are at the same time members of different collectives.

3   The Approach of Economics

Economics or catallactics, the only branch of the theoretical sciences of human action that has up to now been elaborated, views the collectives as creations of the cooperation of individuals. Guided by the idea that definite ends sought can be attained either better or only by cooperation, men associate with one another in cooperation and thus bring forth what is called groups or collectives or simply human society.

The paragon of collectivization or socialization is the market economy, and the fundamental principle of collective action is the mutual exchange of services, the *do ut des* ["I give so that you give"]. The individual gives and serves in order to be rewarded by his fellow men's gifts and services. He gives away what he values less in order to receive something that at the moment of the transaction he considers as more desirable. He exchanges — buys or sells — because he thinks that this is the most advantageous thing he can do at the time.

The intellectual comprehension of what individuals do in exchanging commodities and services has been obscured by the way in which the social sciences have distorted the meaning of all the terms concerned. In their jargon "society" does not mean the result brought about by the substitution of mutual cooperation among individuals for the isolated efforts of individuals to improve their conditions; it signifies a mythical collective entity in whose name a group of governors is expected to take care of all their fellow men. They employ the adjective "social" and the noun "socialization" accordingly.

Social cooperation among individuals — society — can be based either upon spontaneous coordination or upon command and subordination; in the terminology of Henry Sumner Maine, either upon contract or upon status. Into the structure of the contract society the individual integrates himself spontaneously; in the structure of the status society his place and functions — his duties — are assigned to him by those in command of the social apparatus of compulsion and oppression. While in the contract society this apparatus — the government or the state — interferes only in order to quell violent or fraudulent machinations to subvert the system of mutual exchange of services, in the status society it keeps the whole system going by orders and prohibitions.

The market economy was not devised by a master mind; it was not first planned as an utopian scheme and then put to work. Spontaneous actions of individuals, aiming at nothing else than at the improvement of their own state of satisfaction, undermined the prestige of the coercive status system step by step. Then only, when the superior efficiency of economic freedom could no longer be questioned, social philosophy entered the scene and demolished the ideology of the status system. The political supremacy of the supporters of the precapitalistic order was annulled by civil wars. The market economy itself was not a product of violent action — of revolutions — but of a series of gradual peaceful changes. The implications of the term "industrial revolution" are utterly misleading.

4   A Remark about Legal Terminology

In the political sphere the violent overthrow of the precapitalistic methods of government resulted in the complete abandonment of the feudal concepts of public law and the development of a new constitutional doctrine with legal concepts and terms unknown before. (Only in England, where the transformation of the system of royal supremacy first into that of the supremacy of a caste of privileged landowners and then into that of representative government with adult franchise was effected by a succession of peaceful changes,[6] was the terminology of the *ancien régime* for the most part preserved while its original meaning had long since become devoid of any practical applicability.) In the sphere of

6. It was not the revolutions of the seventeenth century that transformed the British system of government. The effects of the first revolution were annulled by the Restoration, and in the Glorious Revolution of 1688 the royal office was merely transferred from the "legitimate" king to other members of his family. The struggle between dynastic absolutism and the parliamentary regime of the landed aristocracy continued during the greater part of the eighteenth century. It came to an end only when the attempts of the third Hanoverian king to revive the personal regime of the Tudors and the Stuarts were frustrated. The substitution of popular rule for that of the aristocracy was — in the nineteenth century — brought about by a succession of franchise reforms.

civil law the transition from precapitalistic to capitalistic conditions was brought about by a long series of small changes through the actions of people who lacked the power to alter formally the traditional legal institutions and concepts. The new methods of doing business generated new branches of law that were developed out of older business customs and practices. But however radically these new methods transformed the essence and the meaning of the traditional legal institutions, it was assumed that those terms and concepts of the old law that remained in use continued to signify the same social and economic conditions they had signified in ages gone by. The retention of the traditional terms prevents superficial observers from noticing the full significance of the fundamental changes effected. The outstanding example is provided by the use of the concept of property.

Where there by and large prevails economic self-sufficiency of every household, and consequently there is for the much greater part of all products no regular exchange, the meaning of property in producers' goods does not differ from the meaning of property in consumers' goods. In each case property serves the owner exclusively. To own something, whether a producers' good or a consumers' good, means to have it for oneself alone and to deal with it for one's own satisfaction.

But it is quite a different thing in the frame of a market economy. The owner of producers' goods is forced to employ them for the best possible satisfaction of the wants of the consumers. He forfeits his property if other people eclipse him by better serving the consumers. In the market economy property is acquired and preserved by serving the public and is lost when the public becomes dissatisfied with the way in which it is served. Private property in the factors of production is a public mandate, as it were, which is withdrawn as soon as the consumers think that other people would employ it more efficiently. By the instrumentality of the profit-and-loss system, the owners are forced to deal with "their" property as if it were other people's property entrusted to them under the obligation to utilize it for the best possible satisfaction of the virtual beneficiaries, the consumers. All factors of production, including also the human factor, viz., labor, serve the totality of the members of the market economy. Such is the real meaning and character of private property in the material factors of production under capitalism. It could be ignored and misinterpreted only because people — economists and lawyers as well as laymen — had been led astray by the fact that the legal concept of property as developed by the juridical practices and doctrines of precapitalistic ages has been retained unchanged or only slightly altered after its effective meaning had been radically altered.[7]

It is necessary to deal with this issue in an analysis of the epistemological problems of the sciences of human action because it shows how radically the approach of modern praxeology differs from that of the traditional older ways of studying social conditions. Blinded by the uncritical acceptance of the legalistic doctrines of precapitalistic ages, generations of authors entirely failed to see the characteristic features of the market economy and of private ownership of the means of production within the market economy. In their view, the capitalists and entrepreneurs appear as irresponsible autocrats administering economic affairs for their own benefit without any regard for the concerns of the rest of the people. They depict profit as unfair lucre derived from the "exploitation" of the employees and the consumers. Their passionate denunciation of profit prevented them from realizing that it is precisely the necessity to make profits and to avoid losses that forces the "exploiters" to satisfy the consumers to the best of their abilities by supplying them with those commodities and services they are most urgently asking for. The consumers are sovereign because they ultimately determine what has to be produced, in what quantity, and of what quality.

5   The Sovereignty of the Consumers

One of the characteristics of the market economy is the specific way in which it deals with the problems offered by the biological, moral, and intellectual inequality of men.

In the precapitalistic ages the superior, i.e., the smarter and more efficient individuals, subdued and enthralled the masses of their less efficient fellows. In the status society there are castes; there are lords and there are servants. All affairs are managed for the sole benefit of the former, while the latter have to drudge for their masters.

In the market economy the better people are forced by the instrumentality of the profit-and-loss system to serve the concerns of everybody, including the hosts of inferior people. In its frame the most desirable situations can be attained only by actions that benefit all the people. The masses, in their capacity as consumers, ultimately determine everybody's

7. See Mises, *Die Gemeinwirtschaft* (2nd ed.; Jena, 1932), pp. 15 ff. (English-language translation *Socialism* [Yale University Press, 1951 (reprint, Indianapolis, Ind.: Liberty Fund, 1981)], pp. 40 ff.)

revenues and wealth. They entrust control of the capital goods to those who know how to employ them for their own, i.e., the masses', best satisfaction.

It is, of course, true that in the market economy not those fare best who, from the point of view of an enlightened judgment, ought to be considered as the most eminent individuals of the human species. The uncouth hordes of common men are not fit to recognize duly the merits of those who eclipse their own wretchedness. They judge everybody from the point of view of the satisfaction of their desires. Thus, boxing champions and authors of detective stories enjoy a higher prestige and earn more money than philosophers and poets. Those who bemoan this fact are certainly right. But no social system could be devised that would fairly reward the contributions of the innovator whose genius leads mankind to ideas unknown before and therefore first rejected by all those who lack the same inspiration.

What the so-called democracy of the market brings about is a state of affairs in which production activities are operated by those of whose conduct of affairs the masses approve by buying their products. By rendering their enterprises profitable, the consumers shift control of the factors of production into the hands of those businessmen who serve them best. By rendering the enterprises of the bungling entrepreneurs unprofitable, they withdraw control from those entrepreneurs with whose services they disagree. It is antisocial in the strict meaning of the term if governments thwart these decisions of the people by taxing profits. From a genuinely social point of view, it would be more "social" to tax losses than to tax profits.

The inferiority of the multitude manifests itself most convincingly in the fact that they loathe the capitalistic system and stigmatize as unfair the profits that their own behavior creates. The demand to expropriate all private property and to redistribute it equally among all members of society made sense in a thoroughly agricultural society. There the fact that some people owned large estates was the corollary of the fact that others owned nothing or not enough to support them and their families. But it is different in a society in which the standard of living depends on the supply of capital goods. Capital is accumulated by thrift and saving and is maintained by abstention from decumulating and dissipating it. The wealth of the well-to-do of an industrial society is both the cause and the effect of the masses' well-being. Also those who do not own it are enriched, not impoverished, by it.

The spectacle offered by the policies of contemporary governments is paradoxical indeed. The much defamed acquisitiveness of promoters and speculators succeeds daily in providing the masses with commodities and services unknown before. A horn of plenty is poured upon people for whom the methods by means of which all these marvelous gadgets are produced are incomprehensible. These dull beneficiaries of the capitalistic system indulge in the delusion that it is their own performance of routine jobs that creates all these marvels. They cast their votes for rulers who are committed to a policy of sabotage and destruction. They look upon "big business," necessarily committed to catering to mass consumption, as upon the foremost public enemy and approve of every measure that, as they think, improves their own conditions by "punishing" those whom they envy.

To analyze the problems involved is, of course, not the task of epistemology.

CHAPTER 7

The Epistemological Roots of Monism

1   The Nonexperimental Character of Monism

Man's world view is, as has been pointed out, deterministic. Man cannot conceive the idea of an absolute nothing or of some thing originating out of nothing and invading the universe from without. The human concept of the universe comprehends everything that exists. The human concept of time knows neither of any beginning nor of any end of the flux of time. All that is and will be was potentially present in something that was already existing before. What happens was bound to happen. The full interpretation of every event leads to a *regressus in infinitum* [process of tracing an event back endlessly step by step].

This unbroken determinism, which is the epistemological starting point of all that the experimental natural sciences do and teach, is not derived from experience; it is a priori.[1] Logical positivists realize the aprioristic character of determinism and, faithful to their dogmatic empiricism, passionately reject determinism. But they are not aware of the fact that there is no logical or empirical basis whatever for the essential dogma of their creed, their monistic interpretation of all phenomena. What the empiricism of the natural sciences shows is a dualism of two spheres about the mutual relations of which we know very little. There is, on the one hand, the orbit of external events about which our senses convey information to us, and there is, on the other hand, the orbit of invisible and intangible thoughts and ideas. If we not only assume that the faculty to develop what is called mind was already potentially inwrought in the original structure of things that existed from eternity on and was brought to fruition by the succession of events that the nature

---

1. "La science est déterministe; elle l'est *a priori*; elle posture le déterminisme, parce que sans lui elle ne pourrait être." Henri Poincaré, *Dernières pensées* (Paris, 1913), p. 244.

of these things necessarily produced, but also that in this process there was nothing that could not be reduced to physical and chemical events, we are resorting to deduction from an arbitrary theorem. There is no experience that could either support or refute such a doctrine.

All that the experimental natural sciences up to now have taught us about the mind-body problem is that there prevails some connection between a man's faculty of thinking and acting and the conditions of his body. We know that injuries to the brain can seriously impair or even entirely destroy man's mental abilities and that death, the total disintegration of the physiological functions of the living tissues, invariably blots out those activities of the mind that can be noticed by other people's minds. But we know nothing about the process that produces within the body of a living man thoughts and ideas. Almost identical external events that impinge on the human mind result[,] with different people and with the same people at different moments[,] in different thoughts and ideas. Physiology does not have any method that could adequately deal with the phenomena of the mind's reaction to stimuli. The natural sciences are unable to employ their methods for the analysis of the meaning a man attaches to any event of the external world or to other people's meaning. The materialistic philosophy of La Mettrie and Feuerbach and the monism of Haeckel are not natural science; they are metaphysical doctrines aiming at an explanation of something that the natural sciences could not explore. So are the monistic doctrines of positivism and neopositivism.

In establishing these facts one does not intend to ridicule the doctrines of materialistic monism and to qualify them as nonsense. Only the positivists consider all metaphysical speculations as nonsense and reject any kind of apriorism. Judicious philosophers and scientists have admitted without any reservation that the natural sciences have not contributed anything that could justify the tenets of positivism and materialism and that all these schools of thought are teaching is metaphysics, and a very unsatisfactory brand of metaphysics.

The doctrines that claim for themselves the epithet of radical or pure empiricism and stigmatize all that is not experimental natural science as nonsense fail to realize that the allegedly empiricist nucleus of their philosophy is entirely based upon deduction from an unwarranted premise. All that the natural sciences can do is to trace back all the phenomena that can be — directly or indirectly — perceived by the human senses to an array of ultimately given data. One may reject a dualistic or pluralistic interpretation of experience and assume that all these ultimate data might in the future development of scientific knowledge be traced back to a common source. But such an assumption is not experimental natural science. It is a metaphysical interpretation. And so is the further assumption that this source will also appear as the root out of which all mental phenomena evolved.

On the other hand, all the attempts of philosophers to demonstrate the existence of a supreme being by mundane methods of thinking, either by aprioristic reasoning or drawing inferences from certain observed qualities of visible and tangible phenomena, have led to an impasse. But we have to realize that it is no less impossible to demonstrate logically by the same philosophical methods the nonexistence of God or to reject the thesis that God created the x from which everything the natural sciences deal with is derived and the further thesis that the inexplicable powers of the human mind came and come into being by reiterated divine intervention in the affairs of the universe. The Christian doctrine according to which God creates the soul of every individual cannot be refuted by discursive reasoning as it cannot be proved in this way. There is neither in the brilliant achievements of the natural sciences nor in aprioristic reasoning anything that could contradict Du Bois-Reymond's *Ignorabimus* ["we do not know"].

There cannot be such a thing as scientific philosophy in the sense that logical positivism and empiricism ascribe to the adjective "scientific." The human mind in its search for knowledge resorts to philosophy or theology precisely because it aims at an explanation of problems that the natural sciences cannot answer. Philosophy deals with things beyond the limits that the logical structure of the human mind enables man to infer from the exploits of the natural sciences.

2   The Historical Setting of Positivism

One does not satisfactorily characterize the problems of human action if one says that the natural sciences have — up to now, at least — failed to provide anything for their elucidation. A correct description of the situation would have to stress the fact that the natural sciences do not even have the mental tools to become aware of the existence of such problems. Ideas and final causes are categories for which there is no room left in the system and in the structure of the natural sciences.

Their terminology lacks all the concepts and words that could provide an adequate orientation in the orbit of the mind and of action. And all their achievements, however marvelous and beneficial they are, do not even superficially touch the essential problems of philosophy with which metaphysical and religious doctrines try to cope.

The development of the almost generally accepted opinion to the contrary can easily be explained. All metaphysical and religious doctrines contained, besides their theological and moral teachings, also untenable theorems about natural events that, with the progressive development of the natural sciences, could be not only refuted but frequently even ridiculed. Theologians and metaphysicians stubbornly tried to defend theses, only superficially connected with the core of their moral message, which to the scientifically trained mind appeared as most absurd fables and myths. The secular power of the churches persecuted scientists who had the courage to deviate from such teachings. The history of science in the orbit of Western Christianity is a history of conflicts in which the doctrines of science were always better founded than those of the official theology. Meekly the theologians had finally in every controversy to admit that their adversaries were right and that they themselves were wrong. The most spectacular instance of such an inglorious defeat—perhaps not of theology as such, but certainly of the theologians—was the outcome of the debates concerning evolution.

Thus originated the illusion that all the issues theology used to deal with could be one day fully and irrefutably solved by the natural sciences. In the same way in which Copernicus and Galilei had substituted a better theory of the celestial movements for the untenable doctrines supported by the Church, one expected future scientists to succeed in replacing all other "superstitious" doctrines by "scientific" truth. If one criticizes the rather naive epistemology and philosophy of Comte, Marx, and Haeckel, one ought not to forget that their simplism was the reaction to the even more simplicist teachings of what is today labeled Fundamentalism, a dogmatism that no wise theologian would dare to adopt any longer.

Reference to these facts in no way excuses, still less justifies, the crudities of contemporary positivism. It merely aims at a better understanding of the intellectual environment in which positivism developed and became popular. Unfortunately, the vulgarity of positivistic fanatics is now on the point of provoking a reaction that may seriously obstruct mankind's intellectual future. Again, as in the late Roman Empire, various sects of idolatry are flourishing. There are spiritualism, voodoo, and similar doctrines and practices, many of them borrowed from the cults of primitive tribes. There is a revival of astrology. Our age is not only an age of science. It is also an age in which the most absurd superstitions are finding credulous adepts.

3   The Case of the Natural Sciences

In view of these disastrous effects of a beginning excessive reaction against the excrescences of positivism, there is need to repeat again that the experimental methods of the natural sciences are the only ones adequate for the treatment of the problems involved. Without discussing anew the endeavors to discredit the category of causality and determinism, we have to emphasize the fact that what is wrong with positivism is not what it teaches about the methods of the empirical natural sciences, but what it asserts about matters concerning which—up to now at least—the natural sciences have not succeeded in contributing any information. The positivistic principle of verifiability as rectified by Popper[2] is unassailable as an epistemological principle of the natural sciences. But it is meaningless when applied to anything about which the natural sciences cannot supply any information.

It is not the task of this essay to deal with the claims of any metaphysical doctrine or with metaphysics as such. As the nature and logical structure of the human mind is, many a man is not satisfied with ignorance concerning any problem and does not easily acquiesce in the agnosticism in which the most fervent search for knowledge results. Metaphysics and theology are not, as the positivists pretend, products of an activity unworthy of Homo sapiens, remnants of mankind's primitive age that civilized people ought to discard. They are a manifestation of man's unappeasable craving for knowledge. No matter whether this thirsting after omniscience can ever be fully gratified or not, man will not cease to strive after it passionately.[3] Neither positivism nor any other doctrine is called upon to condemn a religious or metaphysical tenet that does not contradict any of the reliable teachings of the a priori and of experience.

2. See above, p. 68–69.
3. "L'homme fait de la métaphysique comme il respire, sans le vouloir et surtout sans s'en douser la plupart du temps." E. Meyerson, *De l'explication dans les sciences* (Paris, 1927), p. 20.

4   The Case of the Sciences of Human Action

However, this essay does not deal with theology or metaphysics and the rejection of their doctrines by positivism. It deals with positivism's attack upon the sciences of human action.

The fundamental doctrine of positivism is the thesis that the experimental procedures of the natural sciences are the only method to be applied in the search for knowledge. As the positivists see it, the natural sciences, entirely absorbed by the more urgent task of elucidating the problems of physics and chemistry, have in the past neglected and may also in the near future neglect to pay attention to the problems of human action. But, they add, there cannot be any doubt that once the men imbued with a scientific outlook and trained in the exact methods of laboratory work have the leisure to turn toward the study of such "minor" issues as human behavior, they will substitute authentic knowledge of all these matters for the worthless palaver that is now in vogue. "Unified science" will solve all the problems involved and will inaugurate a blissful age of "social engineering" in which all human affairs will be handled in the same satisfactory way in which modern technology supplies electric current.

Some rather significant steps on the way to this result, pretend the less cautious harbingers of this creed, have already been made by behaviorism (or, as Neurath preferred to call it, behavioristics). They point to the discovery of tropisms and to that of conditioned reflexes. Progressing further with the aid of the methods that brought about these achievements, science will one day be able to make good all the promises of positivism. It is a vain conceit of man to presume that his conduct is not entirely determined by the same impulses that determine the behavior of plants and of dogs.

Against all this impassioned talk we have to stress the hard fact that the natural sciences have no intellectual tool to deal with ideas and with finality.

An assured positivist may hope that one day physiologists may succeed in describing in terms of physics and chemistry all the events that resulted in the production of definite individuals and in modifying their inborn substance during their lives. We may neglect raising the question whether such knowledge would be sufficient to explain fully the behavior of animals in any situation they may have to face. But it cannot be doubted that it would not enable the student to deal with the way in which a man reacts to external stimuli. For this human reaction is determined by ideas, a phenomenon the description of which is beyond the reach of physics, chemistry, and physiology. There is no explanation in terms of the natural sciences of what causes hosts of people to remain faithful to the religious creed in which they were brought up and others to change their faith, why people join or desert political parties, why there are different schools of philosophy and different opinions concerning a multiplicity of problems.

5   The Fallacies of Positivism

Consistently aiming at an improvement of the conditions under which men have to live, the nations of Western and Central Europe and their scions settled in overseas territories have succeeded in developing what is called — and more often smeared as — Western bourgeois civilization. Its foundation is the economic system of capitalism, the political corollary of which is representative government and freedom of thought and interpersonal communication. Although continually sabotaged by the folly and the malice of the masses and the ideological remnants of the precapitalistic methods of thinking and acting, free enterprise has radically changed the fate of man. It has reduced mortality rates and prolonged the average length of life, thus multiplying population figures. It has, in an unprecedented way, raised the standard of living of the average man in those nations that did not too severely impede the acquisitive spirit of enterprising individuals. All people, however fanatical they may be in their zeal to disparage and to fight capitalism, implicitly pay homage to it by passionately clamoring for the products it turns out.

The wealth capitalism has brought to mankind is not an achievement of a mythical force called progress. Neither is it an achievement of the natural sciences and of the application of their teachings for the perfection of technology and therapeutics. No technological and therapeutical improvements can be practically utilized if the material means for its utilization have not been previously made available by saving and capital accumulation. The reason why not everything about the production and the use of which technology provides information can be made accessible to everybody is the insufficiency of the supply of capital accumulated. What transformed the stagnant conditions of the good old days into the activism of capitalism was not changes in the natural sciences and in technology, but the adoption of the free enterprise principle. The great ideological movement that started with the Renaissance, continued in the Enlightenment, and in the nineteenth century culminated in Liberalism[4] produced both capitalism — the free market economy — and its political corollary or — as the Marxians have to say, its political "superstructure" — representative government and the individuals' civic rights: freedom of conscience, of thought, of speech, and of all other methods of communication. It was in the climate created by this capitalistic system of individualism that all the modern intellectual achievements thrived. Never before had mankind lived under conditions like those of the second part of the nineteenth century, when, in the civilized countries, the most momentous problems of philosophy, religion, and science could be freely discussed without any fear of reprisals on the part of the powers that be. It was an age of productive and salutary dissent.

A countermovement evolved, but not from a regeneration of the discredited sinister forces that in the past had made for conformity. It sprouted from the authoritarian and dictatorial complex deeply inwrought in the souls of the many who were benefited by the fruits of freedom and individualism without having contributed anything to their growing and ripening. The masses do not like those who surpass them in any regard. The average man envies and hates those who are different.

What pushes the masses into the camp of socialism is, even more than the illusion that socialism will make them richer, the expectation that it will curb all those who are better than they themselves are. The characteristic feature of all utopian plans from that of Plato down to that of Marx is the rigid petrification of all human conditions. Once the "perfect" state of social affairs is attained, no further changes ought to be tolerated. There will no longer be any room left for innovators and reformers.

In the intellectual sphere the advocacy of this intolerant tyranny is represented by positivism. Its champion, Auguste Comte, did not contribute anything to the advancement of knowledge. He merely drafted the scheme of a social order under which, in the name of progress, science, and humanity, any deviation from his own ideas was to be prohibited.

4. The term *Liberalism* as employed in this essay is to be understood in its classical nineteenth-century connotation, not in its present-day American sense, in which it signifies the opposite of everything that it used to signify in the nineteenth century.

The intellectual heirs of Comte are the contemporary positivists. Like Comte himself, these advocates of "Unified Science," of pan-physicalism, of "logical" or "empirical positivism," and of "scientific" philosophy did not themselves contribute to the advancement of the natural sciences. The future historians of physics, chemistry, biology, and physiology will not have to mention their names and their work. All that "Unified Science" brought forward was to recommend the proscription of the methods applied by the sciences of human action and their replacement by the methods of the experimental natural sciences. It is not remarkable for that which it contributed, but only for that which it wants to see prohibited. Its protagonists are the champions of intolerance and of a narrow-minded dogmatism.

Historians have to understand the political, economic, and intellectual conditions that brought about positivism, old and new. But the specific historical understanding of the milieu out of which definite ideas developed can neither justify nor reject the teachings of any school of thought. It is the task of epistemology to unmask the fallacies of positivism and to refute them.

CHAPTER 8

Positivism and the Crisis of Western Civilization

1   The Misinterpretation of the Universe

The way in which the philosophy of logical positivism depicts the universe is defective. It comprehends only what can be recognized by the experimental methods of the natural sciences. It ignores the human mind as well as human action.

It is usual to justify this procedure by pointing out that man is only a tiny speck in the infinite vastness of the universe and that the whole history of mankind is but a fleeting episode in the endless flux of eternity. Yet the importance and significance of a phenomenon defies such a merely quantitative appraisal. Man's place in that part of the universe about which we can learn something is certainly modest only. But as far as we can see, the fundamental fact about the universe is that it is divided into two parts, which — employing terms suggested by some philosophers, but without their metaphysical connotation — we may call *res extensa* ["a thing which has spatial extent"], the hard facts of the external world, and *res cogitans* ["a thing of thinking"], man's power to think. We do not know how the mutual relations of these two spheres may appear in the vista of a superhuman intelligence. For man their distinction is peremptory. Perhaps it is only the inadequacy of our mental powers that prevents us from recognizing the substantial homogeneousness of what appears to us as mind and as matter. But certainly no palaver about "unified science" can convert the metaphysical character of monism into an unassailable theorem of experiential knowledge. The human mind cannot help distinguishing two realms of reality, its own sphere and that of external events. And it must not relegate the manifestations of the mind to an inferior rank, as it is only the mind that enables man to cognize and to produce a mental representation of what it is.

Positivism's world view distorts the fundamental experience of mankind, for which the power to perceive, to think, and to act is an ultimate fact clearly distinguishable from all that happens without the interference of purposive human action. It is vain to talk about experience without reference to the factor that enables man to have experience.

2   The Misinterpretation of the Human Condition

As all brands of positivism see it, the eminent role man plays on the earth is the effect of his progress in the cognition of the interconnectedness of natural — i.e., not specifically mental and volitional — phenomena and in its utilization for technological and therapeutical behavior. Modern industrial civilization, the spectacular affluence it has produced, and the unprecedented increase in population figures it has made possible are the fruits of the progressive advancement of the experimental natural sciences. The main factor in improving the lot of mankind is science, i.e., in the positivistic terminology, the natural sciences. In the context of this philosophy society appears as a gigantic factory and all social problems as technological problems to be solved by "social engineering." What, for example, is lacking to the so-called underdeveloped countries is, in the light of this doctrine, the "know-how," sufficient familiarity with scientific technology.

It is hardly possible to misinterpret mankind's history more thoroughly. The fundamental fact that enabled man to elevate his species above the level of the beasts and the horrors of biological competition was the discovery of the principle of the higher productivity of cooperation under a system of the division of labor, that great cosmic principle of becoming. What improved and still improves the fecundity of human efforts is the progressive accumulation of capital goods without which no technological innovation could ever be practically utilized. No technological computation and calculation would be possible in an environment that would not employ a generally used medium of exchange, money. Modern industrialization, the practical employment of the discoveries of the natural sciences, is intellectually conditioned by the operation of a market economy in which prices, in terms of money, for the factors of production are established and thus the opportunity is given to the engineer to contrast the costs and the proceeds to be expected from alternative projects. The quantification of physics and chemistry would be useless for technological planning if there were no economic calculation.[1] What is lacking to the underdeveloped nations is not knowledge, but capital.[2]

The popularity and the prestige that the experimental methods of the natural sciences enjoy in our age and the dedication of ample funds for the conduct of laboratory research are attendant phenomena of capitalism's progressive accumulation of capital. What transformed the world of horse-drawn carriages, sailing ships, and windmills step by step into a world of airplanes and electronics was the laissez-faire principle of Manchesterism. Large savings, continuously in search of the most profitable investment opportunities, are providing the resources needed for rendering the accomplishments of the physicists and chemists utilizable for the improvement of business activities. What is called economic progress is the joint effect of the activities of the three progressive groups — or classes — of the savers, the scientist-inventors, and the entrepreneurs, operating in a market economy as far as it is not sabotaged by the endeavors of the nonprogressive majority of the routinists and the public policies supported by them.

What begot all those technological and therapeutical achievements that characterize our age was not science, but the social and political system of capitalism. Only in the climate of huge capital accumulation could experimentalism develop from a pastime of geniuses like Archimedes and Leonardo da Vinci into a well-organized systematic pursuit of knowledge. The much decried acquisitiveness of the promoters and speculators was intent upon applying the accomplishments of scientific research to the improvement of the masses' standard of living. In the ideological environment of our age, which, driven by a fanatical hatred of the "bourgeois," is anxious to substitute the "service" principle for the "profit" principle, technological innovation is more and more directed toward the fabrication of efficient instruments of war and destruction.

The research activities of the experimental natural sciences are in themselves neutral with regard to any philosophical and political issue. But they can thrive and become beneficial for mankind only where there prevails a social philosophy of individualism and freedom.

1. About the problems of economic calculation, *see* Mises, *Human Action*, pp. 201–232 and 691–711.
2. This answers also the often raised question why the ancient Greeks did not construct steam engines although their physics gave them the theoretical knowledge required. They did not conceive the primary importance of saving and capital formation.

In stressing the fact that the natural sciences owe all their achievements to experience, positivism merely repeated a truism which since the demise of *Naturphilosophie**** nobody any longer disputed. In disparaging the methods of the sciences of human action, it paved the way for the forces that are sapping the foundations of Western civilization.

3　The Cult of Science

The characteristic feature of modern Western civilization is not its scientific achievements and their service for the improvement of people's standard of living and the prolongation of the average length of life. These are merely the effect of the establishment of a social order in which, by the instrumentality of the profit-and-loss system, the most eminent members of society are prompted to serve to the best of their abilities the well-being of the muses of less gifted people. What pays under capitalism is satisfying the common man, the customer. The more people you satisfy, the better for you.[3]

This system is certainly not ideal or perfect. There is in human affairs no such thing as perfection. But the only alternative to it is the totalitarian system, in which in the name of a fictitious entity, "society," a group of directors determines the fate of all the people. It is paradoxical indeed that the plans for the establishment of a system that, by fully regulating the conduct of every human being, would annihilate the individual's freedom were proclaimed as the cult of science. Saint-Simon usurped the prestige of Newton's laws of gravitation as a cloak for his fantastic totalitarianism, and his disciple, Comte, pretended to act as the spokesman of science when he tabooed, both as vain and as useless, certain astronomical studies that only a short time later produced some of the nineteenth-century's most remarkable scientific results. Marx and Engels arrogated for their socialist plans the label "scientific." The socialist or communist prepossession and activities of outstanding champions of logical positivism and "unified science" are well known.

* Mises probably means by *Naturphilosophie* the type of anthropomorphism to which he refers in chapter II, section 2, which held that "God or nature acts in a way not different from the ways of human action."

3. "Modern civilization, nearly all civilization, is based on the principle of making things pleasant for those who please the market and unpleasant for those who fail to do so." Edwin Cannan, *An Economist's Protest* (London, 1928), pp. vi ff.

The history of science is the record of the achievements of individuals who worked in isolation and, very often, met with indifference or even open hostility on the part of their contemporaries. You cannot write a history of science "without names." What matters is the individual, not "team work." One cannot "organize" or "institutionalize" the emergence of new ideas. A new idea is precisely an idea that did not occur to those who designed the organizational frame, that defies their plans, and may thwart their intentions. Planning other people's actions means to prevent them from planning for themselves, means to deprive them of their essentially human quality, means enslaving them.

The great crisis of our civilization is the outcome of this enthusiasm for all-round planning. There have always been people prepared to restrict their fellow citizens' right and power to choose their own conduct. The common man always looked askance upon all those who eclipsed him in any regard, and he advocated conformity, *Gleichschaltung* ["bringing into line, elimination of political opponents"]. What is new and characterizes our age is that the advocates of uniformity and conformity are raising their claims on behalf of science.

4 The Epistemological Support of Totalitarianism

Every step forward on the way toward substituting more efficient methods of production for the obsolete methods of the precapitalistic ages met with fanatical hostility on the part of those whose vested interests were in the short run hurt by any innovation. The landed interest of the aristocrats was no less anxious to preserve the economic system of the *ancien régime* than were the rioting workingmen who destroyed machines and demolished factory buildings. But the cause of innovation was supported by the new science of political economy, while the cause of the obsolete methods of production lacked a tenable ideological basis.

As all the attempts to prevent the evolution of the factory system and its technological accomplishments aborted, the syndicalist idea began to take shape. Throw out the entrepreneur, that lazy and useless parasite, and hand over all the proceeds — the "whole produce of labor" — to the men who create them by their toil! But even the most bigoted enemies of the new industrial methods could not fail to realize the inadequacy of these schemes. Syndicalism remained the philosophy of illiterate mobs and got the approbation of intellectuals only much later in the guise of British Guild Socialism, Italian Fascism's *stato corporativo*, and twentieth-century "labor economics" and labor union politics.[4]

The great anticapitalistic device was socialism, not syndicalism. But there was something that embarrassed the socialist parties from the early beginnings of their propaganda, their inability to refute the criticism that their schemes met on the part of economics. Fully aware of his impotence in this regard, Karl Marx resorted to a subterfuge. He and his followers, down to those who called their doctrines "sociology of knowledge," tried to discredit economics by their spurious ideology-concept. As the Marxians see it, in a "class society" men are inherently unfit to conceive theories that are a substantially true description of reality. A man's thoughts are necessarily tainted "ideologically." An ideology, in the Marxian sense of the term, is a false doctrine, which, however, precisely on account of its falsity, serves the interests of the class from which its author stems. There is no need to answer any critique of the socialist plans. It is fully sufficient to unmask the nonproletarian background of its author.[5]

This Marxian polylogism is the living philosophy and epistemology of our age. It aims at making the Marxian doctrine impregnable, as it implicitly defines truth as agreement with Marxism. An adversary of Marxism is necessarily always wrong on account of the very fact that he is an adversary. If the dissenter is of proletarian origin, he is a traitor; if he belongs to another "class," he is an enemy of "the class that holds the future in its hands."[6]

The spell of this Marxian eristic trick was and is so enormous that even the students of the history of ideas failed for a long time to realize that positivism, following in the wake of Comte, offered another makeshift to discredit economics wholesale without entering into any critical analysis of its argumentation. For the positivists, economics is no science because it does not resort to the experimental methods of the natural sciences. Thus, Comte and those of his followers who under the label of sociology preached the total state could dub economics as metaphysical nonsense and were freed from the necessity to refute its teachings by discursive reasoning. When the revisionism of Bernstein had temporarily weakened the popular prestige of Marxian orthodoxy, some younger members of the Marxian parties began to search in the writings of

4. *See* Mises, *Human Action*, pp. 808–816.
5. *Ibid.*, pp. 72–91.
6. *Communist Manifesto*, I.

Avenarius and Mach for a philosophical justification of the socialist creed. This defection from the straight line of dialectical materialism appeared as sacrilege in the eyes of the uncompromising guardians of the undefiled doctrine. Lenin's most voluminous contribution to the socialist literature is a passionate attack upon the "middle-class philosophy" of empirio-criticism and its adepts in the ranks of the socialist parties.[7] In the spiritual ghetto into which Lenin had confined himself during all of his life he could not become aware of the fact that the Marxian ideology-doctrine had lost its persuasive power in the circles of the natural scientists and that positivism's panphysicalism could render better services in the campaigns to vilify economic science in the eyes of mathematicians, physicists, and biologists. However, a few years later, Otto Neurath instilled into the methodological monism of "unified science" its definite anticapitalistic note and converted neopositivism into an auxiliary of socialism and communism. Today both doctrines, Marxian polylogism and positivism, amicably vie with each other in lending theoretical support to the "Left." For the philosophers, mathematicians, and biologists there is the esoteric doctrine of logical or empirical positivism, while the less sophisticated masses are still fed a garbled variety of dialectical materialism.

Even if, for the sake of argument, we may assume that the rejection of economics by panphysicalism was motivated by logical and epistemological considerations only and that neither political bias nor envy of people with higher salaries or greater wealth played any role in the matter, we must not pass over in silence the fact that the champions of radical empiricism stubbornly refuse to pay any attention to the teachings of daily experience contradicting their socialist predilections. They not only neglect the failure of all "experiments" with nationalized business in the Western countries. They do not care a whit about the undisputed fact that the average standard of living is incomparably higher in the capitalistic countries than in the communist countries. If pressed hard, they try to push aside this "experience" by interpreting it as a consequence of the capitalists' alleged anticommunist machinations.[8] Whatever one may think about this poor excuse, it cannot be denied that it amounts to a spectacular repudiation of the very principle that considers experience as the only source of knowledge. For in the view of this principle,

7. Lenin, *Materialism and Empirio-Criticism* (first published in Russian, 1908).
8. *See* Mises, *Planned Chaos* (1947; reprint ed., Irvington, N.Y.: Foundation for Economic Education, 1977), pp. 80–87. (Reprinted in *Socialism* [new ed., Yale University Press, 1951], pp. 582–589.)

it is not permitted to conjure away a fact of experience by referring to some allegedly theoretical reflections.

5 The Consequences

The outstanding fact about the contemporary ideological situation is that the most popular political doctrines aim at totalitarianism, the thorough abolition of the individual's freedom to choose and to act. No less remarkable is the fact that the most bigoted advocates of such a system of conformity call themselves scientists, logicians, and philosophers.

This is, of course, not a new phenomenon. Plato, who even more than Aristotle was for centuries the *maestro di color che sanno* ["master of those who know" (Dante)], elaborated a plan of totalitarianism the radicalism of which was surpassed only in the nineteenth century by the schemes of Comte and Marx. It is a fact that many philosophers are utterly intolerant of any dissent and want to have any criticism of their own ideas prevented by the government's police apparatus.

As far as the empiricist principle of logical positivism refers to the experimental methods of the natural sciences, it merely asserts what is not questioned by anybody. As far as it rejects the epistemological principles of the sciences of human action, it is not only entirely wrong. It is also knowingly and intentionally undermining the intellectual foundations of Western civilization.

The typeface used in setting this book is Electra, designed in 1935 by the great American typographer William Addison Dwiggins. Dwiggins was a student and associate of Frederic Goudy and served for a time as acting director of Harvard University Press. In his illustrious career as typographer and book designer (he coined the term "graphic designer"), Dwiggins created a number of typefaces, including Metro and Caledonia, and designed as well many of the typographic ornaments or "dingbats" familiar to readers.

Electra is a crisp, elegant, and readable typeface, strongly suggestive of calligraphy. The contrast between its strokes is relatively muted, and it produces an even but still "active" impression in text. Interestingly, the design of the *italic* form — called "cursive" in this typeface — is less calligraphic than the italic form of many faces, and more closely resembles the roman.

This book is printed on paper that is acid-free and meets the requirements of the American National Standard for Permanence of Paper for Printed Library Materials, z39.48-1992. ⊗

Book design adapted by Erin Kirk New, Watkinsville, Georgia, after a design by Martin Lubin Graphic Design, Jackson Heights, New York

Typography by G & S Typesetters, Inc., Austin, Texas

Printed and bound by Edwards Brothers, Inc., Ann Arbor, Michigan